Moors, Dales, Nabs and Wykes

Rambling about the Cleveland Way

The Beginning

In the seventh book of the *Poetics* Aristotle offers a general definition of a plot for a play formulated around a fixed sequence. He says, and I paraphrase, that the beginning mustn't have anything before it, the end mustn't have anything after it, and the middle must come between the beginning and the end. On the face of it one could be forgiven for thinking that great thinkers earned their crusts easily.

The Cleveland Way, rather like Aristotle's plot, has a well defined beginning at Helmsley and an end at Filey which are both marked in sandstone. The middle consists of about 110 miles of path, track and occasionally roads following the western, northern and eastern edge of the North York Moors National Park, in that order.

It always seemed tidier to me to close this loop and indeed the powers that be have seen fit to do just that, designating the Tabular Hills Walk which connects Scalby just north of Scarborough back to the start in Helmsley. Literature on this waymarked route is available from the usual North York Moors National Park Authority outlets.

This book wanders around the Way but isn't a how-to-do-it manual. There is a first class official guide "Cleveland Way" by Ian Sampson (ISBN 1 85410 854 9) and numerous other worthy publications directed at the walker and hiker. This book is a ramble, a kind of meandering along, taking in the path, the scenery and other relevant bits having some relationship to the place, albeit on occasion a tenuous one.

Even more obvious than Aristotle's reflections on the structure of a plot will be this book's copious supply of pictures. Some folk prefer pictures to words and in providing so many perhaps this work will appeal to more people.

The Reformation, the Civil War, alum, jet and ironstone mining, famous vets, gliders, the life forms which thrived along the trail over a hundred million years ago, the life forms – including ourselves – that are there now, the search for 96% of the Universe, the grouse shooters and their quarry and people who will stand in a queue in all weathers outside a fish and chip shop in Whitby: we'll meet them all in the Middle of the Cleveland Way.

The stone marking the beginning of the Cleveland Way in Helmsley

3

The Middle

Helmsley is a busy place with most of the activity in the area around the market place, particularly so on the many weekends that the motor bikers gather for the Bilsdale bike run – a popular adventure for the bikers and one to which the reckless occasionally bring tragedy. In addition Helmsley marks the start of the Cleveland Way, the end of both the Tabular Hills Walk and the Ebor Way as well as both start and end of the Inn Way, which is circular. Needless to say for any of these four Walks and Ways you can start at the end and end at the start, should you be so inclined.

Helmsley Castle is in the care of English Heritage and there are so many of these ruins along the Way that it makes sense to join and save money. Rievaulx Abbey, Byland Abbey, Mount Grace Priory, Gisborough Priory, Whitby Abbey and Scarborough Castle are all either on the walk or within about two miles of it. That there aren't many intact buildings of historical interest along the way is in no small measure due to the work of two Cromwells, Oliver on his own account and the ultimately doomed Thomas (no relation) in his zealous fulfilling of the wishes of his master, Henry VIII.

The state Helmsley Castle finds itself in today reflects more than anything else on the attentions of the members of the Parliamentary army who blew it up after its surrender following a three month siege in 1644. A Tudor mansion forms part of the castle and the whole site is surrounded by a huge moat system. The Rievaulx Terraces (National Trust) with their Doric and Ionic temple follies are just up the Bilsdale Road. This is a popular place for picnics, a stroll, the views of Rievaulx Abbey, Ryedale, and a glimpse of the Cleveland Way through Nettledale.

The neo-gothic monument in the foreground is the work of Gilbert Scott who went on to design the even more elaborate Albert Monument in London. It commemorates the 2nd Baron Feversham.

The Cleveland Way proper starts, appropriately enough, by a car park along Cleveland Way, just off the Bilsdale Road. There lies your track. The distinctive starting marker for the Cleveland Way with the names of some of the places on the path engraved on it is a short distance along the hardcore path.

In Store

The Cleveland Way has been home to many different life forms since our planet cooled off, some of which lived hundreds of millions of years ago. In its time the Way and the area it encloses on three sides has been ocean, swamp, desert and the moorland it is today. The rocks underneath were formed at different times by millions of tiny creatures and the final sculpting is mainly the result of the scouring processes of the last ice age, finished off in parts by the activities of man. It is home to adders, grouse and other moorland birds – I have seen a peregrine at close quarters on the moors – and the moors and woodland traversed by the trail are home to a wide variety of bird and plant life.

The impact of human beings is more obvious on the coastal stretch with its old extractive industry relics and the towns and villages there today. There is only one big town – Scarborough – a couple of smaller ones – Whitby and Saltburn – and the rest are villages of varying sizes, mainly small.

We'll meet evidence of neolithic and bronze age inhabitants who lived along the path. The Romans were here, as were the Angles and Vikings in later years. We pass above the homes of James Herriot and Siegfried Farnon, the Darrowby vets who in real life were Alf Wight and Donald Sinclair. We walk by the sites of crashed World War II bombers and mediaeval battles. We visit the stamping grounds of the forebears of Robert the Bruce of Scotland, the smugglers of the North Yorkshire coast and authors past and present. King William the Conqueror came here in 1069 and reduced the entire region to ashes, with one or two strange and unexplained exceptions. King John is on the path, and Edward II's favourite, Gaveston, met a sticky end in Scarborough. The Quakers had their beginnings near the coastal section. In earlier times it was the home of several of the great financial and religious institutions that were the Cistercian monasteries.

When the weather is good it's great but when it's bad you mightn't see much. You should be aware that the climate on the moors can be very different from that on the plain just a few hundred feet below. One thing is definitely on offer. There isn't a dull mile.

Helmsley Castle Keep – the bit that Cromwell's army left

The start of the Way

In 1644 the view from here would have seen Helmsley Castle, not as now a ruin surrounded by pantile houses but as very much a stout fortification under seige from Thomas "Black Tom" Fairfax, commander of the Parliamentary forces. Thomas, later 3rd Baron Fairfax, suffered a wound during the siege and in recognition of this he was granted the castle, or what was left of it, in 1651.

The castle is surrounded by spectacular earthworks, dug out in Norman times, although the earliest surviving masonry dates from the 12th Century. The castle was able to put up stern resistance to Fairfax. One source I read said that this was the second siege at Helmsley Castle, the first being in 1216 when King John was on the outside with Robert de Ros and his wife Isabel on the inside. Most information nowadays says that the only action the castle saw was in the Civil War.

Fairfax had 700 foot soldiers and 300 cavalrymen stationed to the south of the castle. Sir Gordon Crosland, the commander at the receiving end, managed to hold out for three months. Then the food ran out and shortly afterwards so did the garrison – an attempted relief column was chased along the drovers'

road towards Osmotherley, a path followed nowadays by the Cleveland Way. The royalists were allowed to surrender honourably. Just in case the locals got any ideas about repeating the exercise the castle was wrecked – a legacy Cromwell was to leave across the country. Scarborough Castle got the same treatment, as we will see.

The path rises gently upwards giving pleasant views down across Ryedale and out towards the Wolds. It then takes a sharp left then right along Blackdale Howl Wood which clings to the north bank of the River Rye.

The wood then opens briefly giving a panorama across the valley to the wooded bank opposite before the path passes the abandoned village of Griff, dipping back into woodland and emerging on a metalled road which passes the bottom of the Way to the ruins of Rievaulx Abbey.

Rievaulx isn't on the Way but it isn't far off and it's criminal to miss it.

Looking back to Helmsley from the start of the trek

William's Wooing

We now walk through rolling wooded countryside with gently flowing streams as we make our way past an abandoned mediaeval village towards Rievaulx. This would have looked quite different from how it is today in the period just after the Norman conquest.

William's coronation at Westminster Abbey on Christmas Day in 1066 was merely the end of the first act in his battle to subdue his new kingdom. Anglo-Saxon resistance was a constant thorn in his side, and though not the most famous – Hereward the Wake's in East Anglia is probably the best known – Edgar the Atheling's revolution in the north where he was helped by King Canute's Danish nephew Swein had disastrous consequences for much of North Yorkshire.

The English had taken Durham and besieged York while William was in France. He returned, defeated the English at York and sacked the city. In September 1069, however, Edgar and Swein recaptured York. This time William marched back again, took York and embarked on what has been called the greatest act of genocide in English history. The devastation of vast areas, including much of the countryside around Helmsley, has become

known as the "Harrying of the North" or William's Rough Wooing. The Domesday Book, commissioned by William in order to know how much land was worth so he could raise taxes to pay his restless army, records the ruination of the countryside in monetary terms.

William, known as the bastard (but probably not within his earshot) came to a sticky end at the siege of Mantes in northern France. His horse stumbled over a ditch, the pommel hit his stomach and the internal injuries developed into peritonitis, which took five weeks to kill him. He died in Rouen and was buried at Caen. He was big for his time – Five feet ten and fat, his putrefying body was swollen and he was too big for his tomb. So they tried to squash him in but while they were performing this delicate operation his bloated body burst open. It's said that the smell was horrendous and only a hardy few were able to complete the burial. His remains were thrown out by the Huguenots in 1562. They don't do royal funerals like that any more.

Ryedale between Helmsley and Rievaulx

Griff

The profusion of humps and bumps in the ground near the path mark the site of the mediaeval village of Griff. It is marked on the Ordnance Survey Explorer map of the area. The aforesaid undulations were subject to a detailed survey by English Heritage's Landscape Investigation Team in November and December, 2002. This study revealed that the visible remains appear to date from the monastic period. Griff is somewhat older but there are very few traces remaining of the pre-monastic settlement.

Griff is mentioned in the Domesday Book when it was owned by the King's brother, and may have been the site of a settlement for more than a thousand years. However by 1086 (the year of the Domesday Book) 62 per cent of the area around Rievaulx and Griff was designated as "waste". This furnishes some idea of the devastation dished out by William in his efforts to subdue the area. The village was part of the endowment made to Rievaulx Abbey on its foundation by Walter l'Espec, by this time the landowner, and so it became a property of the abbey, a grange owned by the Cistercians and worked by the lay brothers. The lay brothers did the donkey work for their keep while the monks got on with the hard work of praying for their benefactors. After the dissolution of Rievaulx Griff became part of the Duncombe Estate, which is where it is today.

The boundaries have been identified and remains of what appear to be barns and shelters for farm animals are in evidence. Some of the remnants have been obliterated by ploughing and tracks but parts of the boundary walls are still there, just below the surface.

By 1300 the wasted area of North Yorkshire had been transformed, to no small extent by the Cistercians, into a hive of industry with wool, mining, smelting and salt panning industries. Griff was abandoned by its residents. Wharram Percy, the best known of the ghost villages is is situated just off the Yorkshire Wolds Way. It's thought that this village was abandoned after the Black Death but it is possible that for some of these villages the effects of the plague were compounded by the shift in land use brought about by monasteries changing from agriculture to sheep rearing. Maybe this was the cause of the death of Griff.

13

A Reformer

On many points along the trip we will be reminded of the lasting contribution one man made to the landscape of this country. That man is Henry VIII, "The most unsavoury king. Ever."

Now I know that some people far more knowledgeable than I am will say that Henry did marvellous things with the bureaucracy and that he was a moderniser and it was he who really created the "English" nation despite him being from a Welsh family.

Henry could well have been the inspiration for the ancient Christian Fathers when they codified mankind's fallibilities into the Seven Deadly Sins....

1 Pride – excessive belief in one's own abilities, that interferes with the individual's recognition of the grace of God. It has been called the sin from which all others arise.

2 Envy – the desire for others' traits, status, abilities or situation.

3 Gluttony – an inordinate desire to consume more than that which one requires.

4 Lust – an inordinate craving for the pleasures of the body.

5 Anger – manifested in the individual who spurns love and opts instead for fury.

6 Greed – is the desire for material wealth or gain, ignoring the realm of the spiritual.

7 Sloth – is the avoidance of physical or spiritual work.

There can be no doubt that the monastic institutions carried a great deal of clout. They were rich, powerful and were an integral part of the fabric of life in England from the early twelfth century until they were abolished four hundred years later. They were in many ways a law unto themselves and had accumulated enormous wealth through skilful development of the endowments granted them by rich men trying to squirm through the needle's eye into the Kingdom of Heaven. Henry had his eye on the cash and didn't care about the consequences.

Far be it from me to comment on Henry's physical appearance which is sufficiently well known not to need further elaboration, but at a guess his striking form owed not a little to his multiply deadly lifestyle.

Rievaulx Abbey viewed in the Autumn from the Rievaulx terraces (National Trust owned)

Rievaulx

Rievaulx is probably my favourite ruin. Had it not been for Henry's base requirements then maybe it would be my favourite abbey. As it is, we have to make the best of it. If my assessment of Henry is indeed correct then we can have some idea what lies in store for his soul. The mediaeval scholars have it all planned out for him. The punishments to fit the crimes are:

Pride – broken on the wheel

Envy – put in freezing water

Anger – dismembered alive

Sloth – thrown in snake pits

Greed – put in cauldrons of boiling oil

Gluttony – forced to eat rats, toads, and snakes

Lust – smothered in fire and brimstone

Serves him right.

Henry's requirements for cash to fund his vain profligacy, his quarrel with the Pope and his penchant for women turned out to be the ruination of the country's monasteries, priories and abbeys.

There is no fundamental religious reason why some of the greatest architectural works ever built in this country should now be piles of stones cared for by English Heritage. Henry wanted the money. It's tempting to speculate that Shakespeare may have had Henry in mind when he was describing Hamlet's stepfather, not that he was likely to say so in print.

Rievaulx is a Cistercian ruin which was founded on the instigation of Bernard of Clairvaux. Bernard originally entered Cîteaux – then the Cistercians' only monastery – but moved on to found Clairvaux 1113 with a coterie of the Burgundian ruling class. During his lifetime he oversaw the foundation of 65 new abbeys. Bernard was also heavily involved in the early days of the Knights Templar and hence is the father of a thousand conspiracy theories.

Bernard wrote to Henry I in 1131 to tell him his colonisation of the North of England was about to start and, after provision of land by Walter l'Espec – a commander in Henry I's army – a colony of monks arrived the following year to start work under Abbot William. The abbey grew and prospered during the years 1147 to 1167 under Aelred of Rievaulx when numbers soared and much building work was undertaken.

The view of Rievaulx from the Cleveland Way

Cistercians

The actions of Henry I in acquiescing to Bernard's colonisation also had practical and to some extent philanthropic roots. Henry's father, William the Conqueror, had as we have seen, devastated most of the north of England in the Harrying of the North. The abbey was generously endowed not just by Henry but by the Scottish King David, and no doubt both had one eye to a punishment mitigation plea in the hereafter. Henry looked upon the developments that Bernard would bring through his monasteries as a "Good Thing" which would start the regeneration of the northern part of the kingdom after William's "Rough Wooing".

The Cistercians, a sort of holier-than-thou version of the Benedictines, had a knack of finding some superb locations for their abbeys. The most famous of them is probably Fountains Abbey, a bit too far away to justify inclusion here, but in my opinion Rievaulx is the pick of the bunch which includes other North Yorkshire properties such as Byland (later) and Jervaulx. The setting is probably most famously seen from the National Trust property above the Abbey on Rievaulx Terrace, a Georgian folly providing magnificent views of lower Ryedale. Your first view of the abbey ruins from the Cleveland Way is the one on the previous page. The Abbey lies about a quarter of a mile along the road.

Rievaulx acted as a source for many other abbeys around the country including Warden in Bedfordshire and Melrose in Scotland. By 1300 it was the head of some nineteen other abbeys. Rievaulx's main income derived from sheep and wool, but various factors including disease caused serious problems for the community and by the time Henry Tudor and his pals got to work after the dissolution in 1538 there were only 23 in the community.

Not content with the building project, the Cistercians made substantial alterations to the countryside surrounding the abbey, one example being the diverting of the course of the stream to provide a more convenient supply to their settlement. These industrious monks eventually built up formidable, wealthy and, more to the point from Henry's point of view, undefended enterprises where resistance to asset stripping could be met by butchering a few monks.

Timetable

A Learned Man writes about life at Rievaulx under Aelred.

'He turned the house into a stronghold for the sustaining of the weak, the nourishment of the strong and whole; it was the home of piety and peace, the abode of perfect love of God and neighbour. Who was there, however despised and rejected, who did not find in it a place of rest? Whoever came there in his weakness and did not find a loving father in Aelred and timely comforters in the brethren? When was anyone, feeble in body and character, ever expelled from that house, unless his iniquity was an offence to the community or had destroyed all hope of his salvation? Hence it was that monks in need of mercy and compassion flocked to Rievaulx from foreign peoples and from the far ends of the earth, that there in very truth they might find peace and 'the holiness without which no man shall see God.'

[Walter Daniel, Vita Aelredi: The Life of Aelred of Rievaulx (Oxford, 1978), pp. 36-7.]

This is a timetable from a modern Cistercian monastery.

Morning

4.00	Office of Vigils [Night Office] Personal prayer, meditation, lectio divina
5.30	Office of Lauds [Morning Office], Eucharist, Personal prayer, meditation, lectio divina

[Breakfast as convenient]

8.00	Office of Terce [Third Hour]
8.15	Work, study, interval
11.15	Office of Sext [Sixth Hour]
11.30	Main Meal – with reading
12.00	Siesta

Afternoon

1.40	Office of None [Ninth Hour]
2.00	Work
	Interval
6.00	Office of Vespers [Evening Office]
6.30	Evening Meal – with conversation personal prayer, reading, lectio divina

Sometimes community meetings or conferences

8.00	Office of Compline [Final Office]

But this is a worldly fun filled timetable when we come to compare it to the Carthusians....

Flowers in stone, Rievaulx

Nettle Dale

The Cleveland Way passes along the stone bridge over the river Rye. This bridge replaced the previous one which was destroyed by the great flood of 1754.

The next part of the Cleveland Way is one of the few sections which is on metalled road. It's not for long, though, and we're soon back onto a woodland track on the other side of a wooden gate.

Back along the track, then, and through the gate, we take in a deciduous wooded bank on the left and a couple of ponds on the right which are backed by more deciduous woodland. These ponds were created in order to provide a habitat for wildfowl, and indeed it would appear to be working.

In addition to the ubiquitous mallard the pond hosts teal and pochard together with coots and moorhens. The bright red lifebelt on its post by the big pond is presumably for careless fishermen, wildfowlers or birdwatchers as it is quite obviously too big for the ducks, who seem to be able to manage without lifebelts quite adequately.

I returned in the autumn to take pictures of what I thought would be a spectacular display of yellows, oranges, browns and reds but was a little bit disappointed. The colours seemed to be a mixture of dull greens and browns and the plants on the surface of the pond had gone. The picture wasn't nearly as interesting as this one, taken on the walk proper in May 2003, with all the different shades of greenery and the quiet pond with its surface plants, red lifebelt and ramshackle shack.

The pleasant pathway alongside these two ponds isn't a long one but it is typical English broadleaf woodland with its primroses, anemones, bluebells, cowslips and the rest, depending on the season.

But before we leave the wildfowl to their business, I am reminded of a poacher's tale that was told to me a good few years ago which brings a smile every time I think of it, even now. Shelduck aren't good eating....

Pond in Nettledale

Wildfowl with chips

Back in the 1970s when the pubs were serving basket meals (they can't now because of health and safety regulations) and the height of sophistication was duck a l'orange with Mateus Rose or Liebfraumilch, some friends of ours treated us at their house to a wildfowl meal of birds they'd shot themselves. It was an interesting experience because it was the first time I'd ever eaten anything that hadn't been bought from a shop. By and large it tasted quite good as far as I remember, but as well as being my first encounter with food that had never seen the inside of a fridge, it was well hung, and served with a good burgundy. But not all wildfowl is good eating....

This tale was told to me by my uncle, a shipyard worker and hence in a reserved occupation during the second World War. During the war he was in the home guard and they were on patrol along the sand dunes north of the Tees Estuary, now the Seal Sands heavy chemical complex, having been issued with two rounds of ammunition on condition they didn't use it except in the event of an invasion under pain of court martial. After a while there were two shots and the patrol returned with two ducks, each with a bullet hole neatly planted in the front of each of the birds.

"Where did you get those?" asked their very own Captain Mainwaring.

"Found 'em sir."

"Where's your ammunition?"

"Lost it, sir".

"Lost it?"

"Yes sir."

"What were those bangs?"

"Thunder, sir?"

"Thunder?"

"Must have been, sir"

"Without lightning?"

"Must have blinked, sir"

"Very well, dismiss".

When they got home they put the pan on to cook some chips, prepared the birds for the oven and readied themselves for a rare treat of fresh, whole duck at the height of rationing. Soon there was a horrible smell. They'd got a pair of Shelduck. Shelduck is inedible. I have it at first hand that it tastes of incinerated rubber.

Adder

Leaving the wildfowl to get on with whatever wildfowl do in the way of recreation, the path passes for about a quarter of a mile alongside the stream.

This is an area of mixed woodland and is rather pretty and very quiet, by now well away from the roads and the noise of traffic.

This section of the Cleveland Way is unlike most of the rest which is to a greater or lesser extent along the edge of an escarpment giving extensive views from just about anywhere. From the path above the White Horse at Kilburn it's possible to see over to the Wolds and down to the big power stations in South Yorkshire. Along the path from Sutton Bank you can see right over the plain of Mowbray, past Northallerton and Thirsk right out to the Yorkshire Dales and beyond them, the Pennines. From Roseberry Topping you can see for miles across the Cleveland Plain and the steaming industry along the lower Tees right up over County Durham. And the final half of the Way, along the cliff tops, the view stretches out to the horizon on the North Sea. From the Cleveland Way the boundaries of your view encircle a land area of what I would estimate as about 3000 square miles, or about a sixteenth of the area of England.

But here in Nettledale it's prettier, quieter, sheltered and therefore quite untypical of most of the rest of the walk.

The gate to the centre right of the picture is the path taken by the Cleveland Way. The sign on it reads "Caution. Adders on Bank Sides". We didn't see adders here, but on another trip along the ancient road across Wheeldale – signposted as "Roman Road" but Roman provenance is in some doubt – my young son called me over excitedly because he'd seen a snake. I went over to investigate, and sure enough there was the dark brown diamond zig-zag of the female adder. She wasn't as big as I'd always imagined, but we just stood back and watched her decide that she'd rather be somewhere else and she disappeared off into the heather.

Should you meet one of these shy creatures just leave it alone and it will reciprocate. Bites aren't usually fatal to adults but they are nasty, will make you quite ill and can go gangrenous.

Flassen Wood

The path now strikes up the hill through commercial forestry land and up to Cold Kirby.

The bit through the trees is about as scenic as paths through coniferous woodland ever get, but once out onto the top the views are expansive back across the moors and out towards the wolds.

One thing which I will remember for a long time is the track up through the arable farmland and its inhabitants. There were more dead rats than I have ever seen in one place. And they were about the size of a small terrier. Admittedly this is partly due to the fact that they'd obviously been squashed by some great lumbering piece of agricultural machinery and this tends to exaggerate the size of the creature, but nevertheless it was a fairly impressive sight.

I'm given to understand that one of the attractions for the rodent population is the feed put down for the pheasants. That there is a thriving population of pheasants throughout most of the countryside traversed by the Cleveland Way is beyond doubt. It is also beyond doubt that there are more pheasants shot than can be sold at more or less any price, and these birds can be had for a very reasonable money on the markets and small butchers throughout the season.
It's an ill wind....

The path itself is fairly straight and unspectacular, with the woodland part of it at this time of the year (well into Spring) displaying pretty white flowers and smelling strongly of wild garlic, which is unsurprising because this is what these flowers are. Once out in the open the main interest is in the retrospective unfolding moorland views back to the east which provide an appetite-whetting foretaste of the real thing once the Cleveland Way reaches the high moortops.

The path dips down quite sharply into a gulley and rises just as quickly on the other side, bringing you into the village with the church of St Michael to your left. Cold Kirby, with its wide main thoroughfare, is not unlike many of the villages that lie on the southern side of the North York Moors. The Tabular Hills Walk between Scarborough and Helmsley threads in and out of many of them, most of which provide welcome refreshment, especially on a warm summer's day. Unfortunately Cold Kirby is an exception. It doesn't have a pub.

Cold Kirby

Twenty three place names in Britain start with the word "Cold". Cold Kirby's claim to fame is probably that it had a decoy airfield during the second World War.

The church in the picture is Victorian, dating back to 1841, but it stands on the site of a 12th century church and the font dates to this time.

The church was originally under the control of the Knights Templar, closely related in some ways to the Cistercians down the road at Byland and Rievaulx. After their suppression in 1314 control passed to the Knights Hospitaller, who we'll meet again as we pass along the coast, and they held on until the reformation when Henry got to work.

Cold Kirby was allegedly at one time the home of a concubine to a monk from Byland Abbey – once situated in Old Byland but removed a few miles to the south as we shall see. When the monk, one James Tankerlay, died, his ghost returned to the village, on one visit blowing out the eye of his lover. The abbot was said to have had the corpse dug up and enjoined one Roger Wayneman to dump it in Gormire Lake.

More recently in 1840 the tradesmen to be found there comprised the incumbent vicar, a horse trainer, a stable keeper, an innkeeper, a schoolmaster, a blacksmith and a shopkeeper. There were ten farmers in the parish which is described as being in the wapentake of Birdforth.

In 1890 it is recorded as containing 1620 acres with 124 inhabitants. One Robert Tennant bought the village from the Duncombes and in 1880 sold it to Carl Ferdinand Henry Bolckow of Marton Hall Middlesbrough.

Henry Bolckow has a statue in Exchange Place, Middlesbrough. He arrived as an immigrant in 1841, was at the heart of the iron and steel industry which transformed Middlesbrough from an agricultural backwater to a heavy industrial town, was the town's first mayor, first president of the town's chamber of commerce and, in 1868, became Middlesbrough's first MP.

He died in June, 1878 and over 10,000 people crowded around Marton churchyard for his burial. Marton was the birthplace of James Cook.

Cold Kirby from the Cleveland Way

Hambleton

The Cleveland Way passes through the open spaces of Cold Kirby and out through a path to the left on the outskirts of the village which takes a route through farmland and along the edge of a wood, thence down to the main Thirsk to Scarborough road by the Hambleton Inn. This Inn is the only surviving drovers' inn – the others at Chequers (near Osmotherley) and Dialstone (near the top of Sutton Bank) are now farms, and Limekilns (above Kepwick) is a diminishing pile of stones. Make the best of it – the Hambleton's the last pub until Osmotherley, a stroll of more than thirteen miles.

The area around Hambleton is still busy with the racehorsing fraternity. It is the highest training centre in Britain as well as being one of the oldest and has over 200 acres of natural gallops. In 1740 an Act of Parliament was passed permitting horse racing only at Newmarket, York and Hambleton. Two thirds of legal horse racing in the whole of the country took place within about twenty miles of here. Hambleton was second only to Newmarket. Ascot, Epsom – all the rest are upstarts.

The Hambleton Downs racecourse was at one time the premier racing venue outside Newmarket hosting prestigious races such as the Queen's (or Queen Anne, depending on the source) Gold Cup – originally the Royal Gold Cup – worth at the time the not inconsiderable sum of 100 guineas.

Hambleton races ceased in 1775 but the course is still apparently visible if you know where to look.

When Dorothy Wordsworth passed along here with brother William she recounted a meeting with the drovers, the hardy breed of men who brought their cattle to the markets of England from Scotland.

"...the little Scotch cattle panted and tossed fretfully about," the Scribbler scribbled.

They must have known what was in store for them after Malton market.

The picture is of the path as it makes its way through the short stretch of deciduous woodland before it brings you quite suddenly to a view you are quite likely to remember.

Woodland path between the Hambleton Inn and Sutton Bank escarpment

33

England's finest view

The path emerges from the short woodland section and out in front of you is what local vet Alf Wight used to call "The Finest View in England".

Wainwright may or may not have agreed with him and I suppose we all have our favourites, but it would be hard to disagree that Mr. Herriot may have had a point.

The picture opposite is taken from the spot where we arrive at the cliff edge and it is easy to see what he meant. The Vale of Mowbray spreads expansively beneath with Thirsk in the near distance. Beyond lie the Dales and further afield the Pennines.

The road snaking out from the bottom of the picture is the main A170 from the base of Sutton Bank on its way through Sutton-under-Whitestonecliffe to Thirsk. Incidentally, the Guinness Book of Records has Sutton-under-Whitestonecliffe as the longest place name in England, and it's a bit easier to say and remember than that place in Anglesey.

At this point the first of two spurs on the Cleveland Way (the second is the path to Roseberry Topping) takes in the White Horse of Kilburn. It's only a very short section but the views from it present a whole swathe of the old County of Yorkshire.

The path comes to an end above the White Horse of Kilburn and the view changes from the Pennines first to the great plain of York and then far out over the Vale of Pickering to the Wolds.

With the naked eye on a clear day it is straightforward to make out the towers of York Minster. Further south you can see two or three of the great power station cooling towers belching steam from as far away as Doncaster. It is said that from here, with a pair of binoculars, presumably, you can watch a train leave York station and arrive in Darlington, should you be so inclined and have nothing better to do.

If you cast your eye to the west and look carefully you can see the white domes of the United States spy station at Menwith Hill by the road between Harrogate and Skipton. Along the horizon lie the entrances to the Yorkshire Dales and beyond them the Pennines.

Emerging from the woods to this – between Sutton Bank Top and the White Horse

White Horse

As you wander along the pathway towards the White Horse, looking back you will get a foretaste of the walk to come.

The Cleveland Way follows the line of the cliffs well into the distance, dipping for a brief section into woodland, then out onto the old drovers' road. After another short woodland stretch the limestone is left behind and the change in scenery is marked as we reach the sandstone and shales of the wild moors.

But back here the path passes the end of the runway for the Sutton Bank Gliding Club. If the weather conditions are right you will no doubt get a close up view of the assisted take offs and unassisted landings of these graceful beasts.

At the end of the path is the White Horse of Kilburn, not that you see much of it other than its eyeball from this angle.

This Victorian landmark, visible for miles around, is the work of John Hodgson, a local schoolmaster who organised it, Thomas Taylor, a businessman who financed it and Harrison Weir, an artist who designed it.

It was carved out of the topsoil by 31 men and the exposed scree was whitewashed. No money was left for its upkeep and it has been almost lost on more than one occasion. It was damaged by a hailstorm in 1896 and fell into disrepair after the first World War. Following renovation in 1925, it was in good condition until it was covered up between 1939 and 1946 in order not to give the German bombers an easy bearing. Local man Robert Thompson was prominent in keeping the horse in good condition until his death in 1955. The Kilburn White Horse Association now looks after it in conjunction with the Forestry Commission and the National Park Authority.

Robert "Mouseman" Thompson was born in 1876. After deciding engineering wasn't for him he returned to Kilburn to practice carpentry with particular attention to recreating the skills of the 17th century. Some time before 1920 he was working on a cornice for a screen and he remarked that he was as poor as a church mouse, and he carved one on the screen. It became his trade mark about 20 years later.

Looking North – the Cleveland Way path follows the escarpment

Gliding

I've never been one for much flying. I can see how moving an aerofoil through air can create an upward force which will keep a heavy object airborne. I've seen the diagrams and the calculations and I've proved it to myself by cupping my hand to a wing shape and sticking it out of a car window at 70 mph. I agree, there is one big force upwards, and at 400 mph I accept that it must be very strong. In fact as I walk the Cleveland Way there is ample evidence of it not only from the views of the airliners in the corridor on the way out to the North Atlantic and North America overhead throughout the route, there is also the fright you will get when one of the fighters from RAF Leeming singes your hair on a low pass out of nowhere along the Sutton Bank to Osmotherley path.

But. And it's a big But. Jets have engines pushing them through the air. Propeller planes have propellers pulling them through the air. Gliders don't have either – just a quick tow up there and then they're left to get on with it.

I have the evidence of my own eyes that it does work, and I know, because I'm naturally a trusting person, that it's all to do with air currents and the updraught from the westerly winds catching the precipice at Sutton Bank, but it all seems a bit, well, unscientific, unpredictable and a little bit like "Hoping That Something Will Turn Up". It doesn't seem to me like a reliable way of getting from A to B, but maybe I'm missing the point.

I stand and watch these fragile looking things that you can tip over with one finger getting towed into the air by a stocky little single engine aircraft and something inside me is saying "That thing shouldn't be up there. It's going to fall to bits".

But of course it doesn't and the club height record is an incredible 31,000 ft. You'd have room to spare over Everest. And they manage to get them down, onto a tiny strip of land, in one piece. You only get one chance at it – there's no engine to get you out of trouble if you are going to miss.

You can arrange flights and courses with the club. And I do mean "You". Not my cup of tea, thank you.

Aircraft without engines – gliders get a helping hand at the Sutton Bank Gliding Club

A change of season

Sunlight comprises all the colours of the rainbow – literally. Chlorophyll absorbs red and blue parts reflecting green and so appears green. However it isn't a very stable compound and the action of sunlight actually degrades it, so the plant must manufacture a continuous supply in order to maintain photosynthesis – the series of reactions which, barring a few oddball primitive forms, all life on this planet depends.

Another pigment found in plant leaves is carotene. Carotene is yellow and is also found in carrots, tomatoes and cooked lobster. Carotene absorbs blue-green and blue light, reflecting red, orange, yellow and green and so appears yellow. Together chlorophyll and carotene are responsible for the varying shades of green in plants. Chlorophyll and carotene are both bound to cell membranes called chloroplasts.

A third class of plant pigments are the anthocyanins. Anthocyanins absorb green, blue-green and blue light. However, unlike chlorophyll and carotene, anthocyanins are found in the cell sap. The colour of anthocyanins is dependent on the acidity, or pH, of the soil. At higher pH the anthocyanins appear red, at lower, more acidic pH levels they are more purple. The formation of anthocyanins requires high sugar levels and light, which explains why fruits are green while unripe or ripening and red or purple when ripe, and why the sun turns the sunny side of an apple red.

When the temperature starts to drop in autumn, a woody membrane forms in the leaves of deciduous trees, cutting off the nutrient supply and interrupting the chlorophyll production. The subsequent degradation of the unstable chlorophyll means that the the carotenes are left to colour the leaf, so it goes yellow. However, as the chlorophyll isn't using the sugars to build the plant, the sunlight now promotes the reaction which produces the anthocyanins, turning the leaf's colour to red.

Low temperatures destroy chlorophyll but while it remains above freezing anthocyanins are still being formed. Sunlight enhances the process. So the best autumn colours are formed when dry sunny days are followed by cool dry nights. As in the autumn of 2003 on the Cleveland Way.

Byland

Having rationalised all the mystery and romance of the colours of autumn we return to my friend Henry.

Not actually on the Cleveland Way but only about two miles south-east of the end of the track above the White Horse is the ruined abbey of Byland.

The monks who founded Byland weren't from Yorkshire and they weren't originally Cistercians. They belonged to the order of Savigny which was founded in Normandy around the same time as Bernard founded Clairvaux. The Savigniac monks preceded the Cistercians in England when, in 1124, Stephen Count of Boulogne donated land at Tulketh near Preston, Lancashire. In 1128 for reasons not entirely clear they moved to Furness where the abbey grew successfully, and in 1134 another colony of monks was sent to found an abbey at Calder on the west coast of Cumberland.

In 1138 the Scots invaded and the monks scuttled back to Furness, but not for long, because they were refused entry. So off they went to try their luck with the bishop of York, but on the way they stopped in on Gundrenda de Albini who arranged for them to stay with her relation who was a hermit near Hood, to the east of Thirsk. Word got to the abbot of Furness who tried to claim jurisdiction over the itinerant monks, but they were granted independence by the General Chapter of Abbots in Savigny.

In 1143 they were on the move again, off to the village of Byland, now Old Byland near Cold Kirby. But here they were on Rievaulx's doorstep and the monks of Byland took to complaining that they couldn't stand the continuous noise of the Rievaulx bells.

The community at Byland upped and offed to Stocking, a few miles to the south west, in 1147. But larger forces were at play and for a variety of reasons the Savigny order merged with the Cistercians the same year. The monks acquired the site of the present ruin and by 1165 the first buildings had been completed. The monks made their last move before the Reformation to their new abbey in 1177. The present state of their efforts is probably what you'd expect.

Byland part II

Byland led a quiet existence for most of its 321 year span, only appearing in the history books when it was pillaged by the Scottish army after a victory over the hapless Edward II in 1322.

In 1538 the abbey was surrendered to Henry's Suppression Commissioners, the monks receiving pensions of £6 each and the abbot £50.

The buildings were robbed of anything that was a) valuable and b) removable, the structure left to the elements and the locals to build houses, barns, and, apparently, the local pub.

Byland came into the ownership of the Ministry of Works in 1921 after nearly four hundred years of neglect. It is now in the care of English Heritage.

Byland was a big building complex, the main abbey being early gothic with a large rose window, of which we now see more or less half of the bounding circle.

Inside the ruin there is a surprisingly large section of the tiled floor intact, some of it on view and some still covered by the protecting grass. During the winter the exposed tiles are also covered to afford some protection.

There is a small museum on site which has the artefacts from the excavations which have taken place. There are many detailed stone carvings which once were a feature of the buildings.

With a little imagination, and with the help of the reconstructed imagery to be found on the site, it is possible to get an impression of the scale, detail and craftsmanship that went into the making of the complex. Many, many thousands of man days were devoted to the construction of a marvellous gothic church. To our great loss, Henry was responsible for trashing it, and scores more like it, in the pursuit of his extravagant aggrandisement and wastefulness. His father left the English treasury full, Henry left it empty, despite the plundering of the huge resources of the economic infrastructure that was the monastic system. It must surely be one of the grandest acts of cultural vandalism ever perpetrated in this country.

Byland is a lot less visited than Rievaulx but there is much to see and very helpful and knowledgeable people are there to guide you.

The well preserved tiled floors at Byland

Tree. Leaf.... Missin'

When my eldest child was 20 months old we were out for a toddle along the local beck. He pointed to a tree. Humans are the great communicators from minute zero, and here was the message. "Tree. Leaf." we were informed. Then a pause. "Missin'".

This picture was taken on an unusual day in the autumn when a blanket of fog crowned the whole of the North York Moors while the whole of the rest of the country, seemingly, was bathed in cloudless sunshine. The interior roads and paths on the moors were completely fog bound and the cloud came tumbling down quite spectacularly over the well defined edges of the high ground not only to the west, pictured here from the A170 at the bottom of Sutton Bank, but to the north where the cascade down from Clay Bank resembled a huge waterfall. Unfortunately the high contrasts in the pictures of the tumbling cascade at Clay Bank – white clouds taken into the sun with the dark northern slopes of the hills – render them completely unusable for print.

If nothing else it provides a graphic illustration not to take lightly the warnings about the weather on the Way. The path here is along the escarpment edge. That isn't a great danger on this part of the walk but it's a different story when it comes to the cliffs.

In 1802 William Wordsworth and his devoted sister Dorothy were on their way to Brompton, a village on the A170 not far from Scarborough. The reason for their journey was to visit William's wife-to-be, Mary Hutchinson. The mediaeval barn that was her home has seen many re-incarnations, including one as a tea shop. They passed this spot on the way.

Wordsworth's wanderings and writings got him the coveted job of Poet Laureate in 1843, a year after being granted a Civil List pension of £300 per year.

He was also capable of doggerel with the best of them... Verse III of 'The Thorn' in part:

And to the left, three yards beyond,
You see a little muddy pond
Of water, never dry
I've measured it from side to side:
'Tis three feet long, and two feet wide.

His heart danced with the daffodils and leapt when he beheld a rainbow in the sky. Easy pleased, I suppose. But it was my little lad that got autumn with Tree. Leaf... Missin'.

Autumn mist enveloping the Cleveland Way – the path is in fog, everywhere else is sunny

Gormire

Back along the escarpment from the Sutton Bank National Park Centre the stretch of water beneath you is the only substantial natural expanse of inland water within the North York Moors National Park.

One of the many folk tales and legends involving Gormire tells of a knight who tricked the Abbot of Rievaulx into lending him his white mare. But he couldn't control the horse because she wouldn't respond to his commands. As the pair galloped towards the precipice at Whitestone Cliff the knight heard an unearthly laugh from behind. Still mounted on the mare, the two of them plunged over the cliff into Lake Gormire. He turned just before the final plunge to oblivion to see the Abbot behind him transformed into the devil. Who he managed to tell before he hit the water is unrecorded. Whitestone Cliff is the limestone precipice ahead, carrying the Cleveland Way along its edge. It is also known as White Mare Crag.

Gormire is noted for not having an outlet and legend has it that it is bottomless.

That's as it may, but the geologists tell us that it was formed at the end of the last ice age when the melt water was prevented from escaping by a rather large landslide which blocked the outflow from the lake. The outflow is underneath the water surface.

The centre at the top of Sutton Bank has detailed maps and information about the geology, flora and fauna of the cliff edges together with a few circular walks of varying difficulty and distance. The lake is surrounded by Garbutt Wood, home to badger, fox, deer and squirrels while the lake hosts several wildfowl species.

Looking back along the track the outcrop to the west is Hood Hill. This is near to the spot where the wandering Savigny monks stayed with the hermit on the way to founding Byland Abbey and becoming Cistercians. There are tales of it being used for Druidic sacrifices and there are legends associating it with Robin Hood, who, if all the tales of his exploits in North Yorkshire were even partially true, wouldn't have had much time to fight the Sheriff of Nottingham in Sherwood Forest, Lincoln Green or the Wild Blue Yonder.

Gormire Lake and the Pennines in the distance

49

Wild Blue Yonder

The yonder is blue for the same reason that the sky is blue. The man who took the first steps to explaining why this should be the case was John Tyndall in 1859. He found that by passing white light through a suspension of small particles in water such as very dilute milk or soap the light scattered to the side is bluish while the exit beam is reddened. The scattered light is also partly polarised. This is known as Tyndall Effect or Rayleigh Scattering after the scientist who performed further work on it and refined the equations defining it.

The blue sky and the blue yonder are the result of this scattering. The mathematics which defines the process specifies that the scattering is inversely proportional to the fourth power of the wavelength of the light. This means that the short wavelengths at the violet, indigo and blue ends of the visible light spectrum are subject to much more scattering than the yellow, orange and red at longer wavelengths. We don't see the sky as violet because violet is partly absorbed by the atmosphere and our eyes are not as sensitive to violet as they are to blue. It is incorrect that, as some sources say, the blue of the sky is caused by atmospheric dust and moisture.

The nitrogen and oxygen molecules in the atmosphere are able to scatter the light and Einstein proved it in 1911 by producing the equations explaining the process which agreed precisely with experimental observation.

As the sun is setting its light has to pass through a greater thickness of atmosphere so the shorter wavelengths of light are progressively scattered out of vision. The sky goes to a turquoise, then yellow, orange and red.

The part polarisation of the light can be simply demonstrated by using a pair of polarising sun glasses. Rotating the lenses in front of your eyes varies the amount of light transmitted from the sky and it varies in its intensity.

The air sometimes appears bluer over mountain pine forests because the ozone reacts with the terpenes from the pines to form very small particles that scatter light. Rarely, forest fires or volcanic activity produce bigger particles which scatter red light and let the shorter frequencies through. This happens once in a blue moon.

Back on the Cleveland Way, looking south

Vets

Just under Whitestone Cliff or the White Mare's Crag is the hamlet of Thirlby. This small village was the home of local vet James Alfred Wight, or James Herriot.

The James Herriot books transformed veterinary science in universities, at least for the people wanting to study it. Before the vet books universities were typically offering entrance at a 'C' and two 'D's at 'A' level. With the fame brought by however many books, three feature films and several television series you were lucky to get in with three straight 'A's.

The practice where Alf Wight worked in Kirkgate in Thirsk had been fairly moribund before it was bought by the progressive, thrusting Donald Sinclair – Siegfried Farnon of the Herriot stories. Alf arrived fresh from Glasgow University to work as his assistant shortly afterwards. He stayed with the practice all his working life.

The veterinary practice left 23 Kirkgate in 1996 for a new, purpose-built practice on the southern end of Thirsk and number 23 was bought by Hambleton District Council which now runs it as a museum. The approaches to the area are now signposted as "James Herriot Country". Alf Wight's son James, the author of his father's biography, still works in the practice.

The main characters in the book lived closely together for the rest of their lives, Donald nearby at Southwoods Hall – which you can see from the path – and Brian Sinclair in Harrogate.

Jim Wight's biography – "The Real James Herriot" – makes interesting reading for fans of the James Herriot books, TV series and films. Much of the detail recounted by Jim isn't touched on at all in Alf's writings and the book's style is very much Jim Wight's own. One small snippet of trivial information – Alf Wight wasn't Scottish despite his accent being, in his own words "Glottal Clydeside" – he was born in Sunderland, just up the A19 from here.

Alf Wight died of prostate cancer in 1995 and his son Jim and daughter Rosie decided to scatter their father's ashes "among the moorland grass at the top of the Whitestone Cliffs", alongside where you are walking now.

The White Stone Cliff – final resting place of James Herriot

53

Whither the Weather

Whence the weather is easy. You can see it coming, tracking across the Vale of Mowbray inexorably towards you in big, threatening patches. The rain is on its way and there is nothing you can do about it. If you've been daft and not listened to the sensible people who told you to take warm clothes and a waterproof despite the sunshine then you are going to get well and truly soaked. There is no shelter available. The wind, rain and hail will get you and you will end up cold, drenched and shivering. Welcome to June on the Cleveland Way.

The prevailing winds are of course westerly. The views across the countryside afford plenty of warning of approaching squalls but a fat lot of use it is because for much of the path there isn't anywhere to go but forward or back. The path along the escarpment is easily followed. It's so easy to follow in fact that if you step off much to the left then you fall off the cliff, and the right hand side is scrub, woodland and occasionally dry stone wall. Sideways isn't an option.

"Hill Fort Windy Pit," the remains of an iron age fortification, is to the right of the path among several tumuli dating back to this period of pre-Roman Britain. The North York Moors National Park is peppered with these tumuli, all of which were robbed many years before English Heritage were in a position to do much about it.

The name Windypits derives from the fissures in the limestone which in warm weather are a source for expanding air. On a calm day these gentle breaths of air can agitate the vegetation. There aren't caves to speak of – not like the Dales systems anyway – but the neolithic people who lived here two thousand years ago left traces which tell us that they used these mini-caves for shelter and funeral parlours.

The trees in the picture are near to High Barn farm.

Whither the weather is also easy. It's on its way across the moors to catch the Cleveland Way hikers that thought they'd got away with it as they make their way on the path on the cliff tops along the North Sea coast.

Don't laugh, it's your turn next.

Paradise

Milton wouldn't have recognised it but there again he was blind. Our Paradises are Low and High, not Lost so never Regained.

The path descends from High Barn to Sneck Yate where the metalled road from Boltby to Hawnby reaches its summit from the steep climb. A circular walk back to Sutton Bank can be completed by turning right here then sharp right again along the section of the drovers' road that has been covered in tarmac. The road is straight and boring and seems never ending, the mobile phone mast opposite Dialstone Farm never seems to get any nearer.

But we are on the Cleveland Way so we go straight over the road to continue along the way and down into the woods.

Low Paradise wood is a pleasant, easy path with the viewpoints to the valley below obscured by the broadleaf trees. The track goes downhill for a stretch and there's a convenient spot to the right where a miniature natural amphitheatre with big rocks makes an ideal sheltered spot for a snack and a drink.

Carrying on through the woodland the path starts to rise and joins the tarmac road to High Paradise Farm.

The dogs on the farm will no doubt welcome you as the path takes the left hand side of the buildings and along out to the drovers' road.

The picture opposite is the view that greets you across the open moor to the east, with one of those cheery patches of rain on its way to dampen the spirits of the unprepared.

Turn left along the road to enter another stretch of woodland, this time the edge of Boltby forest, a Forestry Commission plantation. Roe deer, fallow deer and badger inhabit the woodland and the best time to see them is in the early morning or late evening. Buzzards are present and there have recently been isolated reports of red kites — a success story for the re-introduction of these beautiful birds, until recently in Britain confined to a small area in central Wales.

After half a mile or so on the top edge of the woods the path emerges onto the open moor.

Moor-side from Paradise

All Hail

When I started out on this little project I'd already walked the Sutton Bank to Osmotherley stretch but without a camera. With the camera I did it again, but this time in two parts, both circular walks. The first one was from Sutton Bank to the end of the woodland described on the previous page and back to Sutton Bank along the drovers' road.

It had started out fine and dandy along the escarpment but by the time I got to the long straight tarmac section on the way back the sky to the west took on a threatening look.

By the time I got to the turnoff for Old Byland the sky over the fields of rape was quite ugly. Then it started.

The hail was fairly uniform in size – about the size of a pea. There was plenty of it and it came whistling in horizontally. I was well equipped in theory – proper leather, Goretex-lined hiking boots, trousers with Goretex overtrousers, shirt, fleece and Goretex outer jacket. The date was May 12 and the time was 2:30pm.

I turned my back on the onslaught and crabbed sideways along the road. There is no shelter. The hail stung. A lot. All over, but particularly on the back of my neck under my hood and on the back of my head. Then, just when you think it can't get worse, it does. There was a huge crash of thunder and the lightning hit the road. There was no time delay between the lightning and the thunder. It wasn't very far away. I was the highest point within about half a mile.

It's times like this when you need your fairy godmother, and, out of the storm, two of them appeared in a car.

"We don't normally pick men up on the road but in your case we thought we'd make an exception."

If you are reading this then Thank you, dear ladies, thank you, whoever you are.

Sutton Bank car park wasn't far but I've not been more thankful of a lift in a long time. At least the hail was pinging off the car and not off me.

Hail and rape – east of the drovers' road between wherever and Sutton Bank

Drovers Road

In the days before the railways, meat was brought to market on the hoof. The industrial revolution was well under way but the final piece of the jigsaw — the means to feed the new towns and cities — was underdeveloped.

The solution to the problem for the cattle men of Scotland and Wales was to herd their cattle to the English markets and sell the stock there. This part of the old drovers' road has escaped the black tarmac and the only noticeable change in hundreds of years is likely to be the rutting caused by the tracks of the four wheel drive vehicles which occasionally use the track.

This road is very ancient — predating the Romans and even the Bronze Age. Not far from where this picture was taken is a neolithic long barrow, clearly visible to the west of the path shortly after the track emerges from the top of Boltby forest. Most of the tumuli on the North York Moors — and there are over 3000 of them — are from the later Bronze Age. Traces of the characteristic decorated beakers of this lost, 4000 year old civilisation have been found around here.

There is evidence from the pollen types in the Bronze Age relics that the climate of these parts changed for the worse around 500 BC. It would appear that this was the catalyst for the people who lived on this high plateau to make a dive for the more sheltered valleys.

Along the path here to the left are the traces of the old mine workings above Kepwick. Near the top of the road down to this small village there is a pile of stones — all that remains of the old Limekilns Inn. Further along, again to the right of the path, are substantial remains of old quarries and limestone workings.

In his book "James Herriot's Yorkshire" Jim Wight tells of his father's many visits to this spot and he recounts a tale with the grandson of the last landlord of the inn. The Limekilns Inn last had a beer selling licence in 1879.

Droving slowly died the death from about 1850 with the spread of the railways. Cattle were slaughtered near to where they grew and the meat was shifted by the trains. This road is a window in time back to a harder world.

Fence posts by the side of the drovers' road looking south

Halifax

The area around here is the scene of a few air crashes during the second World War. Four of them were Halifax bombers crewed by men from Canada, Australia and England.

On 18th March 1944 a Halifax from Croft aerodrome near Darlington crashed on the moor top above Kepwick when returning from a mine-laying mission to Heligoland. All eight Canadian crew were killed. The pilot was David Evans of Toronto, aged 20.

Two of the crashes took place near Whitestone Cliff above Southwoods Hall, later the home of Donald Sinclair, the Siegfried Farnon of James Herriot's vet books.

The first of these two happened on 4th December 1944. While on a night training exercise practicing low level bombing on the moors a Halifax from Marston Moor crashed carrying a crew from Australia, Canada and England. Two of the seven crew survived, but the pilot, 20 year old Australian Graeme McGrath, wasn't one of them.

About six weeks later on 14 January 1945, a Halifax with Canadian crew crashed nearby after another night training exercise killing all but one of the crew, the rear gunner, who was seriously injured suffering multiple fractures. He was rescued by a Mr Sharp, a civilian from nearby Dialstone Farm, who was decorated for his bravery. Another Canadian, 20 year old John Walsh from Montreal, was the pilot.

On January 18th 1944 a Topcliffe-based Halifax bomber clipped its wing flying too low in thick fog on Black Hambleton and crashed nearby. All the Canadian crew were killed. A cross has been placed as a memorial. The pilot was 22 year old Joseph Pierre Lavalee of Quebec. They were buried in Stonefall cemetery, Harrogate.

The Handley Page Halifax was a four engined bomber looking at first glance a bit like the more famous Lancaster. Unlike the Lancaster, which was more or less exclusively used as a heavy bomber, the Halifax had other duties as a glider tow, coastal command reconnaissance and mine laying work.

The Lancaster was changed to the longer ranged Lincoln to cope with Pacific duties and the Lincoln was developed into the Shackelton maritime reconnaissance plane which served in the RAF until replaced by the US built AWACS in the early 1990s.

The Rambler

"He called me a louse and said, Think of the grouse
Well I thought but I still couldn't see
Why old Kinder Scout and the moors round about
Couldn't take both the poor grouse and me
He said, All this land is my master's
At that I stood shaking my head
No man has the right to own mountains
Any more than the deep ocean bed"

Ewan MacColl, father of the late Kirsty MacColl and partner of Peggy Seeger, wrote plays and wrote and collected many songs during his 74 year life – one in his collection was "Scarborough Fair" of which more, later. His own songs include "The First Time Ever I Saw Your Face", "Freeborn Man", "Shoals of Herring" and the one this is taken from, the "Manchester Rambler".

Written in 1933 as part of the mass Kinder Scout trespass – a confrontation between landowners and hikers – and attached to a theme adapted from Haydn's 94th symphony, it has been around for so long and so often that it's often thought of as traditional folklore. So much so that MacColl, a collector of folk songs, actually "collected" a version of it from Canada which claimed to be a traditional lumberjack tune (I'm a logger, I'm a logger from old BC way).

In the mid 1970s Manchester comedian, folk singer, banjo player and rambler Mike Harding wrote a spoof version which he called the "Manchester Camper" which in these more politically correct days he probably wouldn't have got away with without something of a fuss.

The "Manchester Rambler" is still sung where two or three anoraks are gathered together in his name, especially after a few beers, but it's hard to imagine that he didn't have a tongue-in-cheek aside for the poor rambler.

"I once loved a maid, a spot-welder by trade
She was fair as the rowan in bloom
And the blue of her eye matched the blue moorland sky
And I wooed her from April to June
On the day that we should have been married
I went for a ramble instead
For sooner than part from the mountains
I think I would rather be dead"

As my kids would say – sad or what?

Looking back along the path alongside Black Hambleton – in late August heather

Oakdale

The path skirts the shoulder of Black Hambleton and descends along a rough track at the top of the Crabtree Bank plantation – a coniferous industrial forest.

At the bottom – near the car park on the Osmotherley to Hawnby road – the path leaves the drovers' road and dips down over Jenny Brewster's spring along a flagged, pitched path to woodland and Oakdale.

The reservoirs were built in 1891 and 1910 in order to supply water to Northallerton but were downgraded in the early 1990s and their levels lowered. It is still maintained by the water company and its stock is available to supply compensating water to Cod Beck reservoir, which is up the hill on the Osmotherley to Swainby road and whose car park is the favoured starting point for hikers who are taking on the Lyke Wake Walk.

Black Hambleton marks the end of the limestone rocks and the start of the sandstone....

As a preparation for this book I decided I'd read up on the geology of the area in a proper, intelligent way so I bought "British Regional Geology – Eastern England from the Tees to the Wash". Easy. Not quite. The book is written in a different language. One sentence, more or less at random...

Until recently the Cenomanian of the Southern Province was divided into a lower zone of Schloenbachia varians and a higher zone of Holaster subglobosus, succeeded by a zone or subzone of Actinocamax plenus corresponding to the Plenus or Belemnite Marls at the top of the lower Chalk, and placed by different authorities in the Upper Cenomanian or the basal Turonian.

I suppose if you know what they're on about then it must be highly enlightening. I haven't a clue what it means, or even whether it's about anything within about four light years of the Cleveland Way. All I know is that in the book it's opposite a photograph of Flamborough Head.

Oakdale reservoir through the woodland

Green

A Brazilian friend of mine, now resident in Los Angeles, was on his first visit to the English countryside. "But it's so… green", he said. And of course, it is. For the most part.

We live with it and don't notice but even after two weeks in Spain we can get back and, if we take a few seconds to take it in, this country is, well, green.

Traditionally, landscape photographers are less than enthusiastic about green. The first thing is that you can't get away from it and secondly the end product, particularly in prints, is, shall we say, often uninspiring. Depending on the film stock or printing setup greens can have an unreal electric bluish tinge or can look muddy and dull. It's very difficult to get greens to look like they do in real life.

As mentioned during the little diversion around Tyndall Effect, the "white" light we see is composed of all the colours of the rainbow, but the predominance and spread of these colours varies and is measured by "colour temperature". This is given in degrees Kelvin (same as centigrade but instead of the freezing point of water you add on just over 273 to give the temperature above absolute zero). The colour temperature is the "colour" of the light spectrum that a truly black object would radiate when heated to that temperature. You see it when a blacksmith heats steel – it glows a dull red, then bright red, orange and then yellow as it gets hotter. The change in colour balance is due to the colour temperature of the light increasing. Daylight has a colour temperature of about 5400K (ie bluish) and ordinary domestic room lighting is about 3200K. (ie orange). The electronics in today's digital cameras will try to guess the colour balance for you in order to take into account the different types of lighting. Hopefully the digital rendition here will be reasonably true to life, but it has been very slightly "tweaked" in the software to try to redress the alterations made by the camera's electronics, which will see far too much green in the automatic setting and will try to compensate, dulling the greens in the process.

The trees in the picture are part of the mixed woodland just to the west of the reservoirs.

Early summer greenery in Oakdale

Beck

The wild open moorland and the expansive views are behind us for a couple of miles while we dip down into woodland and then up the other side into the village of Osmotherley.

Having clambered up from the beck along the woodland track and an unmetalled road used by the water company and the reservoir fishermen, the path ambles amiably along for a short stretch on the Osmotherley-Hawnby road as it makes its way to the old drovers' inn at Chequers.

The start of the Lyke Wake Walk, of which more later, is along the road which we'll cross again at Sneck Yate. When the nights are long much of this is done in the dark and some folk have been known to top themselves up with a final beer and a bit of Dutch courage in the Queen Catherine in Osmotherley. Whether that's a good idea I'm not so certain although once you get on the moor top in a howling gale in the middle of the night with 42 miles of tramp ahead of you then it'd be quite an achievement to fall asleep. Unless, of course, you have hypothermia, and that is another issue entirely.

Just up the Swainby road before the reservoir there's an old mill that is now a Youth Hostel. Nearby you'll find the Cote Ghyll camping and caravan site, which is very handy if you're looking for accommodation. The Mill closed for business in 1915.

The path tracks over a meadow and down into the little ravine which is home to the beck. Over the footbridge and there's a tasty little climb up the wooded banks on the Osmotherley side of the stream. This is a little beauty of a scramble to finish the section if you've come from Sutton Bank, tacked on to the end as if in spite, just to sicken you off as you congratulate yourself on finishing what has been a largely level walking section of the Cleveland Way.

At last we make our way into the little pantiled houses, shops and pubs of Osmotherley through a couple of narrow stone gateways (sheep snecks) installed to prevent sheep getting to the pub and begging pints from thirsty ramblers.

Tree on the way down to the beck just outside Osmotherley

Osmotherley

There are lots of short circular walks which take in the area around this little beck and there are some old stone buildings, long abandoned, not far from the Youth Hostel on a little woodland pathway. They look like they were domestic dwellings – maybe for mill workers.

The village's origins go back at least as far as the Saxons. Originally agricultural, it grew in the 18th and 19th centuries with the workers from the alum and jet industries.

St Peter's church in the village was substantially "improved" by the reforming Victorians, but the porch is 15th century and there are parts of it which date from the 12th. It was built on the site of an earlier Saxon church. Osmotherley also lays claim to the world's oldest Methodist chapel, built in 1754. John Wesley stood on the stone table in the centre of the village to preach on his many visits to the village.

Osmotherley's name probably derives from the old Norse Asmundrelac which appears in the Domesday book. More fancifully there is a rather farfetched account of a young Saxon prince by the name of Osmund who was warned by an astrologer of a curse which would cause him to be drowned. His mother took him up onto Roseberry Topping, not known for its deep water, but a freak storm caused a spring to form and drowned him. His body was buried in Osmotherley which is supposed to mean Osmund lies here.

Not far from here, down on the plain about two miles north of Northallerton, 12,000 Scots were killed at the Battle of the Standard on 22 August 1138 when King David of Scotland, in an attempt to help Matilda, daughter of Henry I, was heavily defeated by the northern barons. It is known as the Battle of the Standard because Thurstan, the archbishop of York, set up a ship's mast tied to a four-wheeled carriage and attached the banners or standards of the saints to it. In order to encourage a positive result the barons left their horses behind so they couldn't retreat. Most of the Scots casualties were down to the English archers.

This picture was taken about half a mile from the Cleveland Way on one of those circular walks.

Osmotherley lit between the showers

Last Chance Saloon

Osmotherley has progressed from being an agricultural community through an expansion due to the requirements of the mining and quarrying industries nearby for labour to its present status which largely depends on the passing tourist and hiking trade, at least for the people who now make a living here. It is a popular village for Teessiders wanting to escape the industry and commerce for an idyllic country residence. Its position just off the A19 makes it an ideal dormitory town for the big conurbations about 10 miles up the road.

One thing is very important about Osmotherley. There are pubs and food outlets here as well as an outdoor shop which may be useful if there's anything you think you might rather have for the rest of the trip. This is not the important thing, though. What's more important is that it's the last pub you'll see on the walk until you get down off the moors once and for all at Slapewath, east of Guisborough on the A171 to Whitby. Kildale is the next village but it hasn't got a pub. Slapewath is 32 miles along the path. If you fancy a pint, now's the time. If you follow the suggested stages in the official guide your next pint in a pub will be more than two days

down the line. The stage breaks that the guide proposes are Helmsley, Sutton Bank, Osmotherley, Clay Bank, Kildale, Saltburn, Sandsend, Robin Hood's Bay, Scarborough and Filey. You have been warned.

The Cleveland Way's route through the village passes through a couple of alleyways like this one until it meets the main marketplace, when it turns right up the Swainby road as far as the signpost on the left which takes it back out onto the escarpment high above Mount Grace Priory and slightly below the still-in-use Lady Chapel.

It was walking along this path to the Lady Chapel in the late 1990s that my wife saw, quite clearly crossing the path in front and disappearing off into the undergrowth to the right, an animal with the face, gait and tail of a cat but the size of a full grown labrador. She's a country girl herself, used to the fauna around the area, and not given to fantasy. What it was, who knows, but by the time she'd called me and we arrived at the track through the gorse where it had gone, there was no trace.

The pathway into Osmotherley market place

Lady Chapel

The Lady Chapel is just off the Cleveland Way.

There is a tale that the chapel was founded by Catherine of Aragon, Henry VIII's first wife, but whether the link is any stronger than the name of the Queen Catherine pub in the centre of Osmotherley is conjecture. What is known is that it was founded in 1515 and built by a spring which was connected by steps to the Mount Grace Priory at the bottom of the hill.

The chapel was granted to John Wilson, last prior of Mount Grace, at the Dissolution but by the end of the sixteenth century it had fallen into disrepair. An effort to restore it during the reign of Charles II was effectively scuppered by the Titus Oates plot and the subsequent overthrow of the Stuarts.

During the mid 1750s John Wesley visited and preached in the Catholic chapel in Osmotherley.

The Franciscans looked after the building until 1832 and organised some pilgrimages there for the recusant community. In 1952 the by then ruined chapel was acquired by Catholic owners and restored by the Eldon and Scrope families.

The Franciscans returned and stayed until 1994. The chapel is now serviced by the Benedictines from Ampleforth Abbey who are based at the small monastery in the Old Hall, Osmotherley.

In order to get to the chapel you should take the path to the right, off the Cleveland Way, and follow the track with its fourteen Stations of the Cross. You should retrace your steps back to Cleveland Way along the same route.

The chapel – seating capacity 32 – is usually open during sensible hours. Should you visit on a Saturday afternoon you may find the 3:30 mass in progress.

There were two burials in the chapel but the possibility that one of them is Margaret Clitherow, the York butcher's wife judicially crushed to death in 1586 for refusing to plead and later secretly buried, cannot be confirmed or refuted. The Clitherow's house in the Shambles in York is now a shrine and open to visitors.

The Lady Chapel – a short distance from the Cleveland Way path

Carthusians

Henry VIII's third cultural legacy by the Cleveland Way lies about a quarter of a mile off the track as the crow flies at the bottom of the hill. The only way to get to it from the Cleveland Way is along the footpath which goes past Chapel Wood Farm and down through the woodland. Should you choose to make the detour the only way back up is the way you went down.

Unlike Rievaulx and Byland, Mount Grace was a Carthusian institution. It was founded in 1398, much later than the Cistercian expansion and is the best preserved of the nine established in England. The order was founded around 1084 by Bruno of Cologne at La Grande Chartreuse near Grenoble. Their first English monastery was built at Witham in Somerset at the instigation of Henry II as part of his penance for the murder of Thomas Becket.

The order wear white robes under black cloaks with hair shirts next to the skin at all times. They observe silence other than when reciting the liturgy. They live their lives in their own one-man cells with their own garden. They have no sight of their fellow monks at all other than when they meet in church or at the Sunday communal meal where conversation is prohibited. Normal meals are delivered to the monks' cells through a right-angled opening so the monk inside does not have sight of the deliveryman. Meat is prohibited except during illness and a bread and water fast is observed on Fridays.

Unsurprisingly the Carthusian Order doesn't have too many adherents and there are now no Carthusian monasteries in England.

In 1535 three Carthusians were the first victims of Henry VIII's requirement for a signature on the Oath of Supremacy. Their trial jury refused to convict them because they bore Henry no malice. The repulsive Thomas Cromwell made them an offer they couldn't refuse. He personally threatened the jury that if they didn't convict the monks then they, the jury, would themselves hang. That had the desired effect and the three Carthusians were executed as traitors, to be followed two months later, just over a week after Thomas More's head hit the deck, by a further three, all six hung, drawn and quartered.

Mount Grace

Mount Grace today is owned by the National Trust but managed and maintained by English Heritage. So if you have membership of either of these organisations you get in for nothing.

The layout of the complex is still quite evident although much of it above foundation level has gone. There were twenty three cells, each with its own small garden. One of these was reconstructed early in the 20th century and this has been re-furnished in the style of the Carthusians, giving a good idea of life there at the beginning of the 15th century.

Entrance to the property is through the gardens and manor house built by Thomas Lascelles in 1654 using stone from the monastic buildings.

Interestingly for the connoisseurs of the mundane, the latrine system survives well enough to follow round in some detail, and the monks built an ingenious system to supply fresh water and dispose of foul. The original spring houses were demolished but reconstructed in the 1960s.

The picture opposite is of the garden of the reconstructed cell. Like the cell itself, effort has been made to create an authentic replica of the garden of the times.

The monastery was dissolved in 1539 and sold off at a knockdown price to Sir James Strangwaies, knight, who passed it down through marriage to the Lascelles family.

Although the Carthusian regime is no doubt not for those uncomfortable with their own company to the exclusion of all others for the duration of their entire lifetime, it has an up side. The one-man living quarters with two rooms on two floors would have been a comparative comfort in mediaeval times particularly as it didn't involve sharing with the livestock. The monks would have been comparatively isolated from the ravages of contagious diseases and they led a quiet, unstressed existence. They had nothing to worry about until Henry came a-calling, then all there was to worry about was whether they could stand the sight of their own insides. It's said that Henry suffered great qualms over his first executions. He soon got over it.

The reconstructed Carthusian cell garden at Mount Grace

Coast to Coast

Back along the path going north and we are joined by the Coast to Coast path which runs from St Bees in Cumberland to Robin Hood's Bay. We part company on the high moor at Bloworth – sometimes spelled Blowarth – Crossing and meet up again near Hawsker for the final few miles of the Coast to Coast.

In a sense the Coast to Coast walk takes in some of the best bits of the Cleveland Way and adds a few that the Cleveland Way misses out – particularly the stretches away from the high spots in quaintly named Fryup Dale and Eskdale around Egton Bridge and Grosmont.

The Coast to Coast walk was the brainchild of fellwalker extraordinaire Alfred Wainwright. It is usually undertaken west to east as is the Lyke Wake Walk which means that among other things the prevailing winds are at your back. Wainwright's biographer Hunter Davies describes him as passionate, witty and generous, a far more complex character than the misanthropic curmudgeonly ex-local authority financial officer we all came to know and recognise.

Wainwright's writings started in 1955 with his first book on the English Lakes. The publishers commented that it was possibly the first totally handwritten (and drawn) book since before Caxton.

Michael Joseph, a part of Penguin publishing, had decided to drop the books from their list. Ten years after the end of the publication a bit of a scramble took place to get them back on the shelves in the original form. A big international publishing house like Penguin didn't really have the will to continue with what is, for them, a small selling speciality market, but for Frances Lincoln publishers, the eventual winners from twenty contenders, it represents something of a jewel in the crown for the company. It ensures the continued availability of these remarkable books, written and drawn with an accountant's passion for accuracy and the fellwalker's love for the hills.

The gorse in this picture is on the path not far from Osmotherley, just before it rises to make its way along Arncliffe Wood, just about the spot that the Coast to Coast joins us.

More moody skies on the path travelling north from Osmotherley

Lyke Wake Walk

Around this part of the track the Coast to Coast and Cleveland Way are joined by the Lyke Wake Walk.

This 42 mile hike was the idea of one Bill Cowley, who wrote a piece in the Dalesman in August 1955 challenging anyone who would to a walk of about 40 miles across the high points of the North York Moors National Park from west to east – Scarth Wood Moor to Wyke Point at Ravenscar.

Four months after the challenge the first walk took place across unmarked moorland. It took thirteen hours and led to the foundation of the Lyke Wake Club. Anyone completing the 42 miles of the now defined route within twenty four hours is entitled to membership.

Many adjectives have been used to describe the experience of completing the Walk but I don't recall "enjoyable" ever being one of them. It's a challenge, a test of endurance, a feat of stamina and lots of other things besides but no-one actually seems to admit to enjoy doing it. It can get a bit obsessional with some folk because there are those who will complete double crossings – there and back without stopping, and even a few whose sanity I would question who do quadruple crossings – a total of 168 miles whose record time stands (at the last I read) at 70 hours and 50 minutes. That distance is about the same as the Cleveland Way and the Tabular Hills Walk put together, the scenery is more or less uniformly wild moorland and even in the middle of June it can mean a good ten hours in darkness. As my mother says, if they're right I know where there's a houseful.

The rather sombre nature of the walk together with its passing hundreds of Bronze Age burial mounds gave rise to the rather tongue in cheek name of the Lyke Wake Walk. The word Lyke is related to Lych as in Lych gate, where a coffin is rested prior to the funeral, and is an ancient word for corpse. The dirgers, as the members of the rather amorphous Lyke Wake Walk Club style themselves, have get togethers (wakes) where mirth is frowned upon. They have adopted as their anthem the Lyke Wake Dirge, last sung for real at a funeral in Kildale in 1800, first mentioned in writing in 1686 as being sung in 1616, but probably much older.

85

Beacons and Signals

The path wends pleasantly along the top of Arncliffe Wood where it eventually runs to a channel between a link fence to the left and a dry stone wall to the right.

The reminder that we haven't left civilisation behind meets us square on with the big microwave relay station by Beacon Hill. Microwaves travel by line of sight and are not refracted as much as are radio waves, so it is necessary for their propagation across large distances to have receivers and transmitters at high points along the way. This one is 982 feet above sea level. As the notice on the fence says, the station lies close to the Lyke Wake Walk and is actually on the Cleveland Way and the Coast to Coast. The notice says that they have tried to keep the size of the aerials to a minimum so as not to detract from the beauty of the National Park.

The path emerges from the ironmongery and the woodland onto a short stretch of moorland, Scarth Wood Moor, which marks the start of the Cleveland Way's progress across the tops of the Cleveland Hills.

The view to the left takes in the Cleveland Plain and to the east, in the distance, is the distinctive 1000 feet cone of Roseberry Topping. This landmark will be visible, on and off, until the Way takes to the cliffs south of Saltburn when the view is blocked by the higher ground of the central moors.

Two great advances in pocket modern technology have helped the walker – the mobile phone and the United States Global Positioning System (GPS). For serious walking they provide an information and communication system which the hiker of the early 1980s could only dream about. For the moment, the mobile phone coverage is fine for just about all of this walk. The battery power nowadays should allow a few days of limited use. Signal triangulation can pinpoint you to a few hundred yards – if you're lucky – provided the phone is switched on. If you take a properly charged mobile phone with you at the start of the day then, should the worst happen, you will be found even if you are in no condition to make the call (or blow your whistle). You've never had it so good.

Scarth Nick

From the top of Arncliffe Wood the Cleveland Way / Coast to Coast / Lyke Wake walk takes a right turn and tracks across the high level with views to the north of steamy Teesside nestling in the Tees Valley and the Cleveland Plain. The path is well defined and there is absolutely no problem following it. After almost three miles from Osmotherley the route reaches Scarth Nick.

Scarth Nick is where the drovers travelling south passed up onto the moors. For us it is a dip and then another climb. When you get to the Swainby to Osmotherley road at the bottom the Cleveland Way takes to the tarmac for all of about twenty yards to the right and then we're back on to a path and into the plantation.

Most of the upland path from now until Kildale is flagged with Yorkshire stone. This has made the going hard under foot but has become necessary to control the erosion from so many feet tramping across the moor and degrading the path, in wet weather, to swamp. The distance from Osmotherley to Bloworth Crossing is not far short of fourteen and a half miles (just over twenty two kilometres for the metrically minded) and almost all of it is shared by the three long distance walks as well as many other short circuit hikes.

The Lyke Wake Walk in particular grew immensely in popularity over a period of about twenty five years with many groups of many people doing sponsored walks for various charities and other causes. By the early 1980s there were upwards of a thousand people on busy weekends tramping across the moor on the Lyke Wake alone. Something had to be done. The National Park Authority decided not to close the path but to issue an appeal, which still stands, for groups of not more than ten to attempt the Lyke Wake.

The solution to the problem here and across the whole of this section as far as Clay Bank was to flag the path with stone. Some hard bitten purists lament this intrusion of manufactured infrastructure but it has to be the only sensible way to deal with what was becoming a quagmire in rain, not an uncommon occurrence despite the Cleveland Way being located in an area with one of the lowest rainfalls in the country, believe it or not.

When we get to Scarborough, or thereabouts, we'll be having a look at one of the suggested derivations of that town's name. Bear Scarth Nick in mind – they may just have something in common.

The path down to Scarth Nick

Woodland

The path crosses the road and into Clain Wood. It is fairly open and in the picture here you can clearly see the Lyke Wake Walk way marker alongside the post carrying the yellow arrow (public footpath) and acorn (national trail – ie the Cleveland Way).

The Cleveland Way has quite a few woodland sections but in the main they are quite cheery and not too long, and what's more they're mainly through deciduous broadleaf. Anyone who has spent hours in the depths of a conifer plantation with the ground dark and bare of the diversity of life to be seen in woods such as this will need little convincing that deciduous is definitely the better option. There is an argument that when the conifers are showing new growth in the spring the prospect is a little more cheerful but I know where I'd rather be.

I've not included many pictures of the woodland sections in this book because, despite how it may seem at the time, once the pictures are in front of you there is little to choose between most of the woodland paths in appearance.

The Lyke Wake Walkers are with us on this stretch and for them this is the only real relief they will get from the high, wild moors that constitute over 90% of their challenge.

In a south easterly direction, where Scugdale meets the moors, there is a series of crags on the northern side at the head of the dale. Scot Crags and Barker's Crags give sport to the rock climber on a jumble of sandstone buttresses and boulders. Less frequented, but a popular option for climbers on a windy day, are the rocks in the woods at the enchantingly named Snotterdale.

The Cleveland Way emerges from the woodland at Scugdale and Huthwaite Green, crosses the road, skirts a short section of woodland, re-enters the woods and then climbs up out of the woods and onto the moor top at Live Moor.

Oh, and if it's raining, it's fun, especially if you're trying to take pictures.

Woodland path

91

Bluebells

Onions aren't necessarily the first thing that come to mind when confronted with this fantastic carpet of blue, shimmering in the sunlight beaming through the tree canopy, but they all belong to the same family, the Liliaceae (lilies, onions and bluebells).

British people are perhaps a little complacent in not recognising that the flowering of bluebells in spring is arguably one of the most interesting annual botanical sights in the world. The bluebell, also called wild hyacinth among about a dozen other things, only grows in north-western Europe, with the British Isles being their main stronghold. In fact Britain is home to at least 20% of the entire world's population of the plant. On days like this a statistic such as that isn't too surprising. They can carpet the ground in suitable woodland almost to the exclusion of other plants. These woods are also good places to find early purple orchids, which flower at the same time, during April and May. In these parts, up north, the main flowering tends to be towards the end of this period, and this particular picture is one of many taken in Clain Wood on 19th May.

Bluebell bulbs used to be considered suitable for eating but we now know that all parts of the plant are, in fact poisonous. The bulbs were a source of a starch substitute for the Elizabethans who used the dried powder in water to stiffen their ruffs. The flowers secrete a sticky substance which was used to attach feathers to arrows and pages to books.

Bluebells are pollinated mainly by bees, which often favour yellow or blue flowers such as bluebells which have a pattern, invisible to humans, but which is striking in the near ultraviolet wavelengths which these insects can see. They provide an important source of nectar for bees, hoverflies and butterflies, although honey bees have developed a method of getting at the nectar without picking up pollen by biting a hole at the base of the flower.

They reproduce with seeds shed from a capsule which take three years before themselves producing seed bearing plants. They also reproduce vegetatively using underground stems, thickened to produce a bulb which is pear shaped and about an inch in diameter.

Cleveland Plain

Through the gaps in the wooded sections grand vistas appear to the north which bring the industrial heartland of the lower Tees into view.

Teesside lies steaming away in the middle distance, its biggest town being Bolckow's Middlesbrough, the "infant Hercules" as Gladstone called it. Middlesbrough was founded as "Port Darlington" to ship out the coal brought down by the new Stockton and Darlington railway from the coal fields of Durham. Its rapid expansion came about as a result of the availability of water, coal and the Cleveland Hills ironstone, discovered in 1850. It gave rise to a steel industry which would see the growth of a town of 150,000 people today from a population of about 25 in 1801. By the time the first blast furnace had been built in 1851 the population was 7600. In 1861 it was 19,000 and ten years later it was 40,000. By the turn of the century the population had more than doubled to 90,000. Today the only steelworks remaining are in Redcar just to the east, and Skinningrove, which is on the Cleveland Way. How long this last steel manufacturing remains is uncertain.

Middlesbrough displaced Stockton, over the river and much older as a town – its market charter was granted by King John – as the main Tees port. With the pinning down of the once movable Newport bridge, ships can no longer reach Stockton.

Much of the steam and light which is now on view belongs to the huge chemical complex that has displaced steel as the main heavy industry on both banks of the lower Tees.

Imperial Chemical Industries was born in 1926 with the merger of several smaller but related companies. This was followed in 1946 by the Wilton development on the south bank of the Tees. Together the pool of expertise that was generated and their requirement for chemical suppliers led to the formation of dozens of smaller chemical companies and the production of a whole swathe of bulk, technical grade and fine chemicals. ICI has long since been broken up but the chemical industry is alive, well and increasingly diversified on Teesside, as you can see.

The Cleveland Plain viewed from a spot between Huthwaite Green and Live Moor

Des Res

A few interesting statistics about Swainby, gleaned from the 2001 census information.

The village then was home to 1753 residents, 24 of whom come under the category of "other economically inactive". 60.2% of the houses are detached. 51.3% of the population of the village are classed as managerial, professional or associate professional. There are 1240 cars and vans for the 1753 residents, of whom 310 are under 16 and therefore ineligible to drive. 44.1% of the housing is "owned outright". 33.4% of the population has to make do with a mortgage, the remainder is rented accommodation, mainly private sector. It may or may not come as a surprise to learn that 13.7% of the village's inhabitants work in "Real estate; renting and business activities". One in 7 of the employed males in Swainby is an estate agent. In short, Swainby is a modern country village.

It was not ever thus. The first documented reference to Swainby is 13th Century but the nearby village of Whorlton merits a mention in the Domesday book when it had 20 serfs and 8 ploughs. Whorlton also has a ruined castle and is the site of a lost mediaeval village.

Swainby had a Premonstratensian priory which was founded late in the reign of Henry II by a lady called Helewise. Her son Ranulphus then had it moved to Coverham in Wensleydale in 1212 (or 1215, depending on the source) as a result, apparently, of a dispute between him and the Swainby Canons. His mother had been buried at Swainby but he had her dug up and re-interred up in Wensleydale.

Swainby would appear to be an Anglo-Saxon / Viking hybrid name meaning Swein's village or residence. As we saw earlier a man with the same name got himself into big trouble with William the Conqueror at York in 1069. Many of the places in this part of the world have names ending in –by, a lasting testament to the influence of the men from the north.

Nowadays it is a pleasant village with a couple of pubs and a stream running down the middle of it, an ideal place for spotting estate agents. Location, location location they say. This would appear to be it.

Looking back along the path at the start of the moorland section at Round Hill

Carlton Moor

The path across the moor top is by now well and truly paved and helpfully crossed by drainage channels. The views to the north over Swainby, Stokesley and, in the distance, Great Ayton at the foot of Roseberry Topping will be a feature of the trail from now more or less until we pass behind the high top over Urra Moor and then it's with us again until we head over the escarpment to Guisborough.

There is more gliding action along the way – Carlton Gliding Club has a runway beside the track just about 5 minutes walk from where this picture was taken. Compared to the gliding station at Sutton Bank this one is in a moonscape with the runway cutting a swathe through the heather. It is wise not to approach the runway but to keep very much to the path – you don't hear them coming.

As we go past the gliding club hangar the path takes a very steep turn downwards to Carlton Bank. Just at the top of the pitched path down there is a sign which reads "Former Mine Working Area. Please Keep to Marked Path".

The mine in question is an old alum mine and there are bits you can fall down. We'll have a look at the whole alum business when we get onto the coastal section but suffice to say at the moment these are the spoils of the old workings as well as the tracks and byways of the old miners. Carlton mine operated from 1680 to 1744.

Down at the bottom of the bank, just before you set back on the trail for the most strenuous part of the walk, there is what might be a welcome stopover at the Lord Stones Cafe. A short walk from there towards the edge and you'll come across the little hang gliding airfield. Airfield seems a bit of a glorification of what in fact is a field, but I'm not sure what else to call it.

At the bottom of the bank lies Carlton village and the pub the Blackwell Ox. This pub is distinguished if for no other reason than its back garden is a camping and caravanning site. You'll need to book in plenty of time – it's always busy. What's more, at the time of writing, it has an excellent Thai chef so the food's a wee bit different from the usual pub fare.

View back from Gold Hill at the start of Carlton Moor

Wainstones I

One theory would have us believe that the Wainstones are so called because apparently they resemble a horse-drawn cart. Be that as it may, but there are those who would perhaps beg to differ. Constable painted a picture of a Hay Wain in 1821 which is now in the National Gallery. In fact it wasn't painted in the rural idyll but in his studio in London from sketches he'd made while out and about in Suffolk. I once knew a man who claimed to be a descendent of John Constable. He was head storeman at a factory which makes PVC flooring. Like all storemen I ever met, he could have intimidated Atilla the Hun. "And Wot do YOU want?". I'd proffer a chit for some piece of equipment or other. "Haven't got none". Then with a cheery flourish you'd be bidden good day in the vernacular of the football terrace. A true artist in the storeman's profession but his medium wasn't the type you could take home to hang on the wall.

Now, it might be me but the jumble of rocks on the top of Hasty Bank bears as much resemblance to a Constable-type hay wain as a shark does, to use a Spike Milligan concept, a "sock full of custard". Exactly how they came to be where they are and to look like they do isn't certain, but it may be that at one time they did indeed look more like a cart than they do now. They are visible for many miles around across the Cleveland Plain, silhouetted against the sky on the western shoulder of Hasty Bank.

They are a popular spot for people messing about in general on the rock faces and for rock climbers who grade them between M(edium) and E4, which is quite difficult apparently. Rock climbing used to be quite a popular pastime at the school I attended, and one of the guys was very good at it. Indeed he was so good that he ended up on Everest. And I do mean ended up – he still hasn't been found. Joe Tasker (for it was he) and Pete Boardman tried to get to the top of Everest in 1982 but they never came back. They tried the lightweight "Alpine" approach and their aim was to do it without oxygen. I was talking to Joe's dad some time later and he told me of his conversation with his son when he first heard this. He said "What next, son? Are you going to do it in your bare feet?"

Joe and Pete Boardman were last seen at the start of the attempt on the Everest East ridge on May 17 1982. Joe was 34, Pete 31.

Wainstones II

The Wainstones also feature in Ewan McColl's "Manchester Rambler" (see "The Rambler" page in this book back at Black Hambleton). In fact the song starts with them. *"I've been over Snowdon, I've slept upon Crowden, I've camped by the Wainstones as well...."*

The view south from the Wainstones is about as different from the northern aspect as it could be.

Looking north there is the huge industrial complex of the lower Tees, south the rural tranquillity of Bilsdale flanked by the highest points of the moorland.

On the road not far south of here there is the village of Chop Gate (pronounced Yat) with its pub. Further south is the Sun Inn, which is a Very Interesting Pub. The modern (well, the pub in current use) isn't the original, which is just behind it. It's one of the oldest buildings still intact within the North York Moors National Park, built about 1550. It was used as a farmworkers' cottage and then a cobbler's workshop before becoming an inn in 1714. It stayed in business, known as the Spout House, until the present pub opened in 1914. It is still very much intact, thatched roof and all, and is the only example I know of an 18th century pub which is now as it was then.

The Bilsdale TV mast is a landmark for many miles around, and indeed can be seen from much of the Cleveland Way and hence gives a good bearing point for compass users when it's not foggy. The grid reference is SE553962 – at least that's the centre of the baseline on the OS map.

Further south before it gets back to Helmsley there is good walking country around Hawnby in the area between the Bilsdale road and the Cleveland Way escarpment trail. The entrance to the Rievaulx Terraces is a couple of miles north of Helmsley.

It would appear that Bilsdale at one time was a wild and scary place – it's said that William had a bit of trouble here in his genocidal wasting and he lost men in a snow storm in the region of Clay Bank.

Moorland

The heather moors are as much a managed landscape as the prairie arable fields of East Anglia. The acid soils covering the sandstones, grits and shales of the northern half of the North York Moors doesn't support the arable crops of the limestone-based south but it is ideal territory for the heathers and lings which grow, assisted, in profusion.

The assistance comes in the form of burning back the old, woody plants in rotation to allow thick growth of new, green shoots. The reason for this is that these shoots form the staple diet of the red grouse, which having dined on the shoots is then itself shot. The tender loving care and careful management ensures that the moorland habitat of Ewan McColl's "poor grouse" is in pristine order, providing a healthy revenue from the individuals and organisations who pay considerable sums to enjoy a day's sport.

The wet heathlands of Britain occur on acidic, nutrient-poor substrates, such as shallow peats or sandy soils with impeded drainage. The vegetation is typically dominated by mixtures of cross-leaved heath Erica tetralix, heather Calluna vulgaris, and grasses, sedges and bog-mosses.

The dominant plant species underfoot within the North York Moors National Park thrive on the acidic soil and give the moorland its brown colour most of the year but this glorious purple bloom in late summer. The North York Moors contains the largest continuous expanse of upland heather moorland in England. Erica tetralix – Sphagnum compactum wet heath is the second most extensive vegetation type on the moor and is predominantly found here on the eastern and northern moors where the soil is less free-draining. Purple moor-grass Molinia caerulea and heath rush Juncus squarrosus are also common in this area.

The different heather varieties have slightly different flowering times which gives an extended life to the moorland's purple phase and also gives a subtle difference in hue at different times. The main variety – the Scotch heather or ling, flowers from August to late in September. The bell heather which has deep purple flowers and the cross-leaved heath which has lighter pink flowers are in bloom from July which gives almost three months of purple relief from the sombre browns of most of the year.

September viewpoint looking south from Hasty Bank

Hasty Bank

After clambering your way through the Wainstones the route is easy and level for just over half a mile along a flagged path with extensive views to both north and south, and then there's a steep drop down the pitched path to the Broughton to Helmsley road, where care is required in the wet. If you lose your footing here then the name of the bank will in all probability reflect the nature of your descent.

You will get some idea of the track from the picture, which also gives a view over the Bilsdale road of the path the Cleveland Way takes up the other side to Carr Ridge and then on to the highest point of the North York Moors at Urra Moor.

The horizon on the picture is your path all the way along and down into the Esk Valley at Kildale.

Most people will be using the Bilsdale road as a break in the walk, and after the strenuous up and downs of the past six miles or so there is no building of any sort for the next 13 miles. The car park about two hundred yards from the summit of Hasty Bank is the usual stopping off point for walkers and during the summer you can get an ice-cream here.

If you go to the car park there's a great viewpoint which will give you sight of the path to come almost as far as Kildale. You'll get an idea of this from the winter picture facing the next page.

Great Broughton is about three miles to the left (north) and Chop Gate about the same distance to the right. Both offer pubs and accommodation. Great Broughton is the bigger of the two, and Stokesley, bigger than either of them, is further up the road from Great Broughton. Lots of farms in the dale offer Bed and Breakfast.

The Bilsdale Hunt lays claim to the oldest Hunt in England, having been founded by the Duke of Buckingham in the 1660s. Other sources say that it boasts the oldest pack of foxhounds, presumably as in institution and not the age of the actual animals. Its first point-to-point was held in 1994.

Clay Bank and the Cleveland Way over Urra Moor. Car park is visible bottom left

Chilly

It isn't very often we get snow nowadays. About a zillion years ago when I was little we seemed to get at least one decent snow session in a winter, in some cases more than one.

This picture was taken on 22nd December 2003 when the one and only snowy day of the second half of the year came and went within a period of less than 24 hours. I decided to nip out and get a snowy picture for this publication before the inevitable thaw and this is it. It was taken from the car park at the top of Hasty Bank just off the Bilsdale road. Mine was the only car there at the time and I succeeded in losing my car keys in the snow. Oh what fun.

Beyond the conifers of the Greenhow plantation lie the arable fields around Ingleby Greenhow and beyond the path of the Cleveland Way above the plain. Roseberry Topping is, as usual, prominent, and Captain Cook's Monument can just be made out on the top of Easby Moor.

To the right of Easby Moor the dip is the Esk Valley. Why Wester, Rose, Farn, Fryup, Thornton, Rye, Riccal, Brans, Newton, Wheel, Bays and so on are dales of the North York Moors and the Esk is often referred to as a valley when the others never are isn't obvious, but the OS is at least consistent in this regard and labels it as Eskdale throughout its length from here to Whitby. The railway line from Middlesbrough to Whitby, the Esk Valley Railway, takes a line through Great Ayton which is to the left of the picture below Roseberry Topping, right along the middle distance to Battersby Junction over to the far right, then reverses direction and heads on down the valley through Kildale, which is on the Cleveland Way and is the first stop along the valley. Flanders and Swan couldn't have done better in their "Slow Train" than use the names of the stations along the way – Great Ayton, Battersby Junction, Kildale, Commondale, Castleton Moor, Danby, Lealholm, Glaisdale, Egton Bridge, Grosmont, Sleights, Ruswarp and Whitby. The line was reprieved under much local pressure after Dr Beeching had fingered it for closure. It would appear to have a reasonable future given the amount of support it now has.

Winter from Hasty Bank car park

A Long Time Ago...

The acidic peat on which the heather grows is only part of the story hereabouts. Scratch the surface and we find a fascinating story which explains why the landscape looks like it does and how it has been sculpted over 250 million years.

About 375 million years ago, after the era when the great British coalfields were trees, this area was a sea. Desert conditions followed and then the Upper Permian Zechstein sea flooded the region. Deposits of potash and salt were formed under "evaporating dish" conditions. We will come to these later on in the walk.

The rocks here are about 150 million years old. They were deposited by huge rivers flowing southwards and the swamps played host to giant cycads, horsetails and monkey puzzle trees. These were fossilised as jet. The plants supported the animal life which at this time was dominated by the dinosaurs. Dinosaur bones are rare here but quite a lot of footprints have been found and samples can be seen in the museum at Whitby. The sandstone formed as a result of this period can be seen in the stone out of which the villages are built and is also the cause of the poor quality of the soil on the moors. The dales are more fertile owing to the presence of shales from the lower Jurassic.

For 65 million years the moors have been rising up to form the hills we see today. The moors are cleft by many dales, often containing a beck or small river which looks far too insignificant to have carved such a big valley. Most of these dales were scoured out by torrents of meltwater from overflowing glacial lakes. Bilsdale and Farndale, among others, were cut by glacial meltwater flowing down from the north.

The Cleveland Dyke is a line of hard igneous rock which was injected into the area 58 million years ago by huge volcanoes erupting on the Isle of Mull. Much of the resulting rock has been quarried for road stone. The sandstones make good building material and were also used for millstones to grind corn. Thin coal seams were formed by the plant life and were mined on a small scale. Rosedale Jurassic ironstone was deposited over 150 million years ago and was dug up in the 70 years between 1856 and 1926.

Mount Grice

The plural of grouse, according to my Scottish partner in lab experiments at university, is not grouse but grice because that's how the royal family pronounce it and it also has a logical parallel with mouse and mice.

Lagopus lagopus scoticus – the red grouse of the moors – is found only in the British Isles. It is the close cousin of the willow grouse which populates similar areas of northern Europe, the main obvious difference between the two being that the willow grouse acquires white plumage during the winter whereas the red grouse stays more or less the same all year long.

There is no doubt whatsoever that you will make the acquaintance of these scatty creatures on many occasions during the trek when they will suddenly decide that you're too close and will scare the wits out of you with their braying cackle and break cover.

It's their fast, direct, low flight that makes them such sport and an attraction for the people with the funds and the skill who are one of the economic mainstays of this part of the world, and without them things around here wouldn't be the same.

If it wasn't for the grice shooters then it's very probable that the moors would have a very different look to the one we see today. The soil isn't of the same quality as the limestone-based Tabular Hills so farming isn't an option. Sheep and the burning of the heather to feed the birds provide the basis of the economy, and the appearance of the countryside is the result. If left to itself the moorland would almost certainly lose the characteristic late summer colouring and the encroaching bracken would mean that spring and summer would be largely green instead of brown and that late summer would be brown instead of purple.

If you're interested in shooting then you're better off (and you certainly will be financially) if you shoot pheasant or partridge. It doesn't have the same social cachet that grice have but it's a good bit cheaper. What's more, pheasant haven't got the brains of the grouse and are thus much more approachable (read easy to hit). And they provide a bit more of a mouthful, if it's your intention to bring the fruits of your sporting endeavour to oven and table.

The moorland proper – the wild path over Urra looking back to Hasty Bank

Top of the moors

And so the track brings us to within a stone's throw of the highest point on the moors.

The trig point on the top of Urra Moor (the white pillar on the horizon here) is on a tumulus at the top of Round Hill and marks 1490 feet up. From here it's downhill. Well, downhill more than uphill but there's a fair bit of both still to come.

Most of the tumuli on the moors like this one are iron age round barrows. We've passed the only exception to the round barrow rule along the route of the Cleveland Way on the path above Kepwick.

All the ancient artefacts from the numerous barrows have long since been raided and whatever they contained removed, undocumented. It all points to a time, between about 1000 and 200BC when these moor tops were home to a substantial population. At the time the now open, barren moors were heavily wooded. Deforestation began with the iron age people, continued under Romans and was pretty much complete by the mediaeval period.

The many crosses and standing stones around the moors have been, on occasion, the basis of theories involving ancient wisdom, long lost secrets, ley lines, Stonehenge, the Great Pyramid of Giza and no doubt alien civilisations.

The mundane truth is that they indicate boundaries or are markers for paths. It's not difficult to see, and is quite obvious that stones run parallel to the track we're walking on. The most famous, Ralph Cross, is more or less in the centre of the moors near the Lion Inn on Blakey Ridge, about 8 miles walk along the ironstone railway from the nearest point on the Cleveland Way. Ralph Cross has been adopted by the National Park as its emblem. However there are many other examples like the one in the foreground of this picture which sit beside the moorland section of the path. Near here there is the cutely misspelled "Stoxla" "Kerby" double post – Stokesley and Kirkbymoorside in modern parlance, and an indicator that at one time this path connected these two places which would have had far more importance commercially than they do now.

The trig point (white in the background) marking the highest point on the North York Moors

115

Park

The North York Moors National Park is 554 square miles of geographically well defined upland. Its borders are the Tabular Hills to the south overlooking the Vale of Pickering, the escarpment to the west rising out of the Vale of Mowbray, the Cleveland Hills to the north looking out expansively over the Tees Valley and to the east the North Sea cliffs.

It contains a huge variety of different landscapes from wild heather moorland to soft green dales, from secluded woodland to the wild sheer cliffs of the Heritage Coast. Bird life is extensive and varied. It is home to the birds of the moors, the sea, woodland, river and arable farmland. There are more ecosystems than you could shake a stick at — moors, peat bogs, streams, shoreline, cliffs — as well as geological sites of national importance.

Man has left traces of his activities from the neolithic to the present — burial sites, old mineworkings, railways both working and abandoned, villages, upland and arable farms, ancient tracks and standing stones, a missile early warning station and some large commercial forestry plantations. Monks and nuns of several religious orders altered the landscape and built their industrial scale religious institutions. The Romans lived here in their coastal forts, signal stations and camps, the best known of these being the one near Cropton.

Rivers and streams run down its dales to the Esk in the north and ultimately to the Humber in the south.

It is home to the North Yorkshire Moors Railway, 18 miles of preserved track running steam engines between Grosmont and Pickering. The railway has featured as Hogwarts Station in Harry Potter and is often used in sets for the television series "Heartbeat", itself set in Aidensfield, the moorland village of Goathland.

There's a lot of it, it's all different, and our path along most of the perimeter, the Cleveland Way, gives a fairly representative sample of the interior.

The National Park was designated in 1952. Its headquarters are in Helmsley and there are two National Park Centres — The Moors Centre at Danby and Sutton Bank Centre which boasts 'the finest view in England'.

Looking North East from Urra Moor. Roseberry Topping is in the distance, its summit about 400ft below us

117

Crossroads

This picture arguably ignores just about all the classical compositional rules but nevertheless I think that there's something about it that works. The bleak moorland which reaches half way up the picture and the fluffy clouds in a blue sky taking up the other half without a soul in the frame gives a good sense of the reality of the wild countryside traversed by the path.

We are now well into the wild heart of the North York Moors. The absence of any shelter is quite obvious and the picture amply illustrates the wisdom of being prepared for bad weather.

The path ahead leads to a crossroads where the Cleveland Way bears left along the track which leads down to Kildale. The level path in the distance crossing the picture is the old ironstone railway which has just climbed up the Ingleby Incline on its way to the now abandoned Rosedale ironstone mines. It follows the contours and veers off back to the left and continues onward into the picture. The path which disappears off to the right is the well worn Rudland Rigg which hugs the high ground to the east of little-visited Bransdale.

Bransdale is clearly visible for quite a distance to the right along this path and is a place where motorised visitors are uncommon. The dale itself isn't signposted from the Helmsley to Pickering road, a conscious decision intended to help preserve its solitude. Views are extensive on a clear day, right down to the Howardian Hills that flank the southern edge of the main Helmsley to Scarborough road.

This quiet valley is home to some rare birds of prey including the merlin, peregrine and short eared owl and has occasionally been the breeding territory of a pair of honey buzzards.

Motor-bound visitors to the moors might be surprised at the clarity of the old moorland paths, but the three walk traffic that this section of the moors generates in terms of footfall ensures that maintenance by the responsible authorities is necessary to combat and prevent the erosion which has spoiled substantial parts of the Lyke Wake Walk particularly in the Blue Man i' the Moss section. The path descends gently to meet one of the more remarkable man made constructions on the North York Moors. We are about to cross the ironstone railway.

Railway

It's difficult to believe that this isolated gate on the moorland tracks is on the site of what, as recently as 1929, was a manned railway crossing.

The ironstone railway started down in the Esk Valley at Battersby Junction, ran along by Ingleby Greenhow and then was hauled up Ingleby Incline by ropes. The way it worked was the full waggons returning from the Rosedale (and the short lived Blakey) ironstone mines were used as counterweights, being lowered on pulleys. At the other end of the system the empty waggons from the valley floor were hauled up as the full ones made the descent. The operation was controlled from a wheel house, the ruins of which are still visible at the top of the incline.

The railway then tracked along the contours above Bransdale, Farndale and Westerdale, crossing Blakey Rigg and ran along the high ridge west of the valley of Rosedale to the mine workings up on the hillside above the village of that name. Rosedale Abbey (it wasn't an abbey but a Cistercian nunnery, hardly anything of which remains) was, from the middle of the 19th century to the end of the first quarter of the 20th a busy industrial mining centre.

The railway was quite a feat of Victorian engineering and is carried along embankments and cuttings for its length. Life here was hard for the railway workers – the remains of cottages at the top of the embankment are still visible.

There were quite obviously no shops or any other form of entertainment for the families living here – they had to walk down the embankment to pick up a train to go to Stokesley, Whitby, Middlesbrough or Stockton. Their children used to go to school in Farndale, taken along in the train on a Monday morning and picked up on a Friday night.

In bad winters the line was impassible, sometimes for weeks, and on more than one occasion, months on end. In the winter of 1889 the snows didn't clear until June and the whistles froze even on the engines in steam.

The line was taken up in 1929 after the last of the mines closed during the industrial upheavals that followed the end of the General Strike. Some thought was given to re-opening it when plans were being considered to convert beautiful Farndale into a reservoir for Hull. Wainwright wasn't very impressed.

What's left of Bloworth Crossing

121

Incline

This particular picture was taken not far from the Cleveland Way, at the top of the Ingleby Incline on the ironstone railway. The Cleveland Way lies a few dozen yards up the hill behind, although the view from the Way isn't as good as this.

The hills opposite in the middle distance are those along which the Cleveland Way has passed since Cold Moor – west of the Wainstones. Below is the arable farming land around Ingleby Greenhow, leading out to the Cleveland Plain beyond. In the distance are the entrances to the Yorkshire Dales, and in the far background we can see the Pennines and the distinctive hulk of Ingleborough on the horizon, some sixty miles from where we now stand.

This is the view to the west, and the view to the north is as impressive with steamy Teesside and the fields of Durham further north.

This is the view of the people who lived in "Siberia", the small group of houses not far away from here at the top of the incline and who looked after the ironstone railway line.

The incline reached a maximum gradient of 1 in 5 and took the empty waggons up 700 feet over less than three-quarters of a mile.

There were some quite spectacular accidents, and the track had several safety devices built into its construction to minimise the potential for catastrophe.

Anyone interested in the story of this remarkable little railway can find out more by reading a great little book published by the Scarborough and District Archaeological Society which is available from the Tourist Office in Helmsley Market Place.

The publication contains a full account of the Rosedale mines and the railway system. It includes many fascinating photographs of the mines in their industrial heyday and the engines and waggons that ran on the line, together with eye witness accounts of the last of the survivors of the enterprise. Standing here it isn't easy to visualise this wild and lonely site as being full of the bustle of steam engines.

The view from the top of the Incline. The Pennines can be clearly seen

Baysdale and down

At Bloworth we part company from the Lyke Wake Walk and the Coast to Coast Walk as they follow the old railway to the Lion Inn on Blakey. Our next pub isn't for quite a bit further – the Fox and Hounds at Slapewath on the Guisborough to Whitby road.

Kildale is the next village and there is a little railway halt on the Middlesbrough to Whitby line.

We go up the track and along, with the Rudland Rigg path to Kirkbymoorside now behind us, past a row of grouse butts with views of Hasty Bank – and further – to the left. Before long we can see Roseberry Topping poking its distinctive peak over the moor tops, the sheer west part of the summit presenting a side-on view.

This cattle grid marks the start of the metalled section of the road down into Kildale. The Kildale road is to the left and down. The other direction takes you down to the Esk Valley and the isolated little hamlet of Baysdale Abbey. Needless to say there is virtually nothing left of Baysdale Abbey as a structure to visit, and needless to say who is responsible. It was a Cistercian nunnery for nearly 350 years from 1190 until 1539 when its time came to surrender to the dissolution

whose aftermath left nothing but a small bridge. Not much else is available about its history as far as I can tell. It would appear that all that's left of the original buildings is that small stone bridge over Baysdale Beck.

Captain Cook's monument atop Easby moor is visible on the picture opposite above the dry stone wall next to the gate. Also in the picture, Roseberry Topping peeks alluringly over the cattle grid waiting to be climbed as a short but sweet out-and-back spur off the path in the next section between Kildale and Slapewath. The cloud of steam billowing into the sky in the distance to the right of the picture is the eyesore otherwise known as the Boulby Potash Mine, which we will closely encounter later on in the march.

The Way makes its transition from hardcore path into tarmac and tracks down to Kildale.

Cattle grid on the path above Baysdale Abbey

Kildale

The path meets the Kildale to Baysdale metalled road and descends by Little Kildale into the village of Kildale down in the valley. There are more extensive views westward along the Way across the Cleveland Plain to the Dales and Pennines.

Kildale is an estate, not just a village. For the past 900 years it has been owned by only three families, and the boundaries have never changed. Today all the farms in Kildale and almost all the houses are still owned by the estate and are let to people who live permanently in the dale. At one time there was jet and ironstone mining, but nowadays the community relies on agriculture and grouse shooting.

St Cuthbert's church is an 1868 rebuild on a site where a church was founded, date unknown but as far as can be gathered it was probably in Saxon times. Viking burials were found beneath the previous church.

The Percy family, some of whose tombs are in the church porch, built a castle here in the 12th century. These powerful earls of Northumberland were, to all intents and purposes, the rulers of the area and feature prominently in Shakespeare's historical plays. The castle was later replaced by a mediaeval manor house which is now reduced to a few stones.

About 1312 the Friars of the Holy Cross started work on an oratory and other buildings for their settlement in the park of Sir Arnold de Percy but work was stopped by Archbishop Grenfield, because it was unclear that this order of mendicants was approved by the pope. There are no traces of the workings left.

The Esk Valley Middlesbrough to Whitby railway is the only year round public transport available, but it isn't particularly frequent, especially outside summer.

The Cleveland Way passes parallel to the railway through the village on the main road, crosses the railway and then up by Bankside Farm. There are the usual good views back over the Esk Valley and out back along the moorland path we've just left.

Kildale, as we've seen, is one of the little railway stations along the Esk Valley Line and it's to the south west of Kildale that the river itself has its source in the steep sided valley just south of the village of Westerdale. The Esk is unusual in this part of the country being a rare example of a natural waterway running west to east. During the last ice age the ice was about 1000 feet thick in these parts and when it melted what we now call Kildale was at the bottom of a very large lake.

The path descending into Kildale and the view back over arable farmland to Hasty Bank

Cook Monument

"In memory of the celebrated circumnavigator Captain James Cook F.R.S. A man of nautical knowledge inferior to none, in zeal prudence and energy, superior to most. Regardless of danger he opened an intercourse with the Friendly Isles and other parts of the Southern Hemisphere. He was born at Marton Oct. 27th 1728 and massacred at Owythee Feb. 14th 1779 to the inexpressible grief of his countrymen. While the art of navigation shall be cultivated among men, whilst the spirit of enterprise, commerce and philanthropy shall animate the sons of Britain, while it shall be deemed the honour of a Christian Nation to spread civilisation and the blessings of the Christian faith among pagan and savage tribes, so long will the name of Captain Cook stand out amongst the most celebrated and most admired benefactors of the human race."

So reads the inscription on this monument to the great navigator and seafarer which *"As a token of respect for and admiration of that great man, this monument was erected by Robert Campion Esqr. of Whitby AD 1827."* It was restored in 1895 by subscription from the readers of the North Eastern Daily Gazette.

Given that we've been able to see this for miles when you actually get there it comes as a bit of a surprise.

The view from the monument atop Easby Moor is once again extensive, Teesside's industries adding to the pastoral setting of Ord's History of Cleveland, written in 1846...

"The prospect from the summit combines at once the extreme of beauty and sublimity. Nature in her loveliest and most majestic attire; mountains, moors, rivers, ocean, with a vast and almost absolute infinity of intermediate scenery; towns, villages, halls, castles, steeples, towers and spires – farmhouses, cottages, and simple huts – with forests, woods, groves, corn field, pastures, hedgerows, greenlanes – these, with sounds and signs of rural life and rural enjoyment, constitute one of the noblest scenes which it is possible for the mind of man to conceive ... it may be doubted, indeed, whether any scene in Europe presents equal diversity and range of prospect."

The monument to Captain Cook on Easby Moor

129

Easby Moor

On the path out of Kildale, where we pass along the side of a field, there was a sign which warned to beware of the bull. They weren't bluffing.

We pass through a conifer plantation and then all of a sudden we're out into the open on the top of Easby Moor. Through the stones on either side of the path we are confronted with the 51 foot high Cook monument a short hop along the path across the moor top.

The view here to the next major landmark is taken from the monument looking along the trail to Roseberry Topping.

This little hill has been in our sights now, on and off, since Black Hambleton, and it's now only a short walk away, although the final scramble to the top is a bit steep. It's far less daunting than it seems, though. The climb from the mini-col is only 166 feet. If you had chosen to start from the car park at Newton-under-Roseberry by the Guisborough to Great Ayton road you would be looking at 750 feet.

The hill itself isn't particularly high – only 1050 feet – 13 feet lower than we are at the monument on Easby. Its distinctive shape, however, gives it the appearance of a mini-mountain and this aspect in my opinion is greatest from the top of the Tees flyover going south on the A19.

Roseberry's distinctive shape is part due to glaciation and part due to man and it is a little unstable. The cliff face on the western side of the summit is the result of a land slip in 1907 which was caused by jet, ironstone and roadstone quarrying. The instability of the hill means that in years to come its appearance will alter again.

Roseberry is now owned by the National Trust which has undertaken bracken control on the land around it and made it a nicer place to be. On summer days there is usually quite a gathering at the top of the hill. It's a popular visiting place for Teessiders and visitors to the area who fancy a bit of a leg-stretch and want to see the view and get a bit of exercise. Unfortunately some of the visitors are graffiti prone and their handiwork disfigures the summit. Sometimes it's quite easy to dislike people.

But we're not there yet.

Roseberry Topping from Captain Cook's monument

131

Bog Day

I bet you didn't know there was an International Bog Day. The Bog may or may not be at the forefront of your everyday consciousness. The bogs referred to below relate not to the North York Moors but Northern Ireland, but as the bog festival is apparently international presumably this neck of the bog is eligible for inclusion in the worldwide Bogfest.

I quote from a UK government press release, 23 July 2003.

"FOR PEAT'S SAKE – LET'S CELEBRATE INTERNATIONAL BOG DAY"

Organiser Geoff McCormick said: *"Bogs are very much part of our own landscape but their conservation value and their beauty are often overlooked. In order to focus public attention on these wet wonderlands the last Sunday in July has been designated as International Bog Day. The aim of the day is to make people more aware of the importance of peatlands and also highlight the issues, which threaten them."*

Mr McCormick said: *"Peatbogs often thought of as worthless wasteland, are in fact very exciting and interesting. You may live close to one or even pass one on your journey to work. They may seem like very dull and uninteresting places, more of a hindrance than anything but this is far from the truth."*

I quite understand that these landscapes are very important in the British Isles and that in many cases they are under threat, principally from the unsustainable factory harvesting of peat for the home gardener. But celebrating an International Bog Festival? The powers that be trying to jolly us along in organised celebration of all things boggy. Come to "The Big Bog Bash". It might be a riot of fun and jollity but I don't think it'll oust Hogmanay.

Common bog cotton (Eriophorum angustifolium) uses a 'snorkel technique', using large air-filled cells in its roots to survive in the oxygen poor environment under the carpet of Sphagnum. Tiny brilliantly coloured 'jewel' beetles use these air spaces as living quarters.

As a Des Res it mightn't be Swainby, but for these little creatures it's home.

Aireyholme Farm

The Cleveland Way follows the conifer woodland, planted after the first World War, down Crockshaw Hill to the Great Ayton to Kildale road, then back up again along Great Ayton Moor to Newton Moor.

At this point there is the second of two out-and-back spurs – the first one took us to the White Horse near Sutton Bank.

This one is a bit more like hard work, but the view at the top is worth the scramble, and a wayside carving reminds you that despite the diversion, you are still on the Cleveland Way.

When you get to the top of the Topping the view south west is more or less the one in the picture here. Aireyholme Farm is at the bottom of the hill. This isn't the first time we've come across James Cook on our travels and it won't be the last.

There is an enormous amount of literature and history about this truly great seaman available for those wanting to find out more. But a few bits and pieces won't come amiss here.

His father was from Roxburgh in the Scottish Borders and he moved to Teesside after the 1715 Jacobite Rebellion where he met and married Grace Pace, a Thornaby girl. They had eight children but only James, the second son, and two daughters Margaret and Christiana survived to adulthood.

To the left of the picture, at the foot of Roseberry Topping is Great Ayton. James Cook senior moved here with his family to work as a bailiff to the Lord of the Manor on Aireyholme Farm when young James was eight years old. He attended school in the centre of the village, a small classroom on the first floor of the building. This little school is now The Captain Cook Schoolroom Museum.

A statue representing Cook as a boy, by the sculptor Nicholas Dimbleby, commissioned by Hambleton District Council and Great Ayton Parish Council, was unveiled on the High Green in 1997.

He left aged sixteen years to work as apprentice to a draper in Staithes.

135

Landscape

It's a truth, universally acknowledged, that a good view rarely makes a good photograph.

The viewpoint from here is no exception. I did my best but the picture is a poor reflection of the view.

A good landscape photograph isn't made by adhering to a strict set of rules. If it was then anybody could do it.

There isn't a better practitioner of the landscape photographer's art working in Britain today than Joe Cornish. There are others – Charlie Waite and Colin Prior to name but two of my own personal favourites – but the difference is that they don't live by the Cleveland Way.

Joe is one of two photographers that get a mention along our track, the other is the remarkable Frank Meadow Sutcliffe who we'll meet in, and either side of, Whitby.

What both these photographers have in common is the painstaking perfectionist's attention to composition and detail. Both are masters not only of the artistic aspect of photography but of the scientific principles that underlie the production of the image. I can think of no other artistic discipline where science is so important – the optics, the light, and in the traditional chemical medium the knowledge of the chemistry and characteristics of film emulsions and developing and printing.

Joe Cornish is not a native of the area. His work takes him all around the world but much of his output is of the countryside which borders the Cleveland Way. His pictures are instantly recognisable as being his work – sometimes I used to wonder whether it was the landscape or Joe Cornish's work that was in the picture, but I now realise that it's both. Most of the shops round here that sell cards, calendars and books have Joe's work for sale. He works with a 5 x 4 inch Ebony field camera mainly with wide angle lenses. If you fancy really splashing out then limited edition prints are available from his galleries.

The nearest Joe Cornish Gallery is in College Square, Stokesley, about four miles from Great Ayton.

Teesside from Roseberry Topping summit

Whither the Wether

Back down the Topping then and across Newton Moor and Hutton Moor with Codhill Heights to your right. This is the very last small part of the moorland section, so say goodbye to the sheep as you pass Highcliffe Farm, not that they're likely to reciprocate.

It isn't very often that sheep warrant much more than a second's thought, docile creatures that they are. The moorland sheep are mainly swaledales. Their tatty appearance is a reflection of the hard life they lead on the moors – it's hard for a girl to look her best when she's been out on the tiles for a year or two. They can get a bit nasty if they've got lambs, though. Unfortunately they don't have much in the way of back-up, and the wethers aren't much of a help. It's all very well glaring and stamping your feet but if all you've got in reserve is a woolly coat and no sharp teeth then you have a bit of a credibility problem. You can see it in their eyes – "if you don't go away I'll... stamp my feet again... and then I'll... run away. You want the lambs? You can have them. They're all yours. Enjoy the curry."

To venture out on a bit of a tangent at this juncture, Denis Healey, one-time Chancellor of the Exchequer, once remarked in a television interview that being attacked on policy by his opponent, the softly spoken and very correct Geoffrey Howe, was "rather like being savaged by a dead sheep". He certainly had a gift for quotable quotes....

One of his others – "The first law of holes – when you're in one, stop digging", also warrants commitment to memory for those many occasions when our own wits leave us lacking at that critical moment. It's him we have to thank for the comment that, as Chancellor, he would "squeeze the rich until the pips squeak", and he it was who clarified "the difference between tax avoidance and tax evasion" as "the thickness of a prison wall".

And as for whither the poor old wether – there's not much demand for his type nowadays.

E2

At about this point we are joined by a very short stretch of another path called the Tees Link.

The Tees Link itself terminates at Highcliffe Nab (next page) and has its other end at Middlesbrough Dock, a total of ten and a half miles. The Tees Link is also part of one of the English sections of the E2 European Route, which in Britain stretches from Stranraer to Harwich. And the British section is only part of the picture. The whole trek stretches 4850 km (or about 3030 miles) from Galway to Nice – it's designated as the Atlantic to Mediterranean walk. The last bit's a mite strenuous. It's the Grande Traverseé des Alpes – a French national trail known as the GR5.

The E2 uses existing trails wherever possible and in Britain the route is the Southern Upland Way between Stranraer and Melrose, then on the St. Cuthbert's Way to Kirk Yetholm, the Pennine Way as far as Middleton-in-Teesdale, the Teesdale Way to Middlesbrough and the Tees Link brings it here, where it follows the Cleveland Way all the way to Filey. From there it becomes the Yorkshire Wolds Way along its full length to Hessle, the Viking Way to Rutland Water, the Hereward Way to Ely, the Fen Rivers Way to Cambridge, Roman Road Link to Linton, Icknield Way Path to Stetchworth, Stour Valley Path to Stratford St. Mary and finally in this country the Essex Way to Ramsey and a short link to Harwich.

The whole E network consists of eleven long distance paths at the moment, and the E2 is slightly shorter than the average. The E1 for instance takes you from well inside the Arctic Circle at the North Cape to Sicily.

The only other one to cross Britain is the E8 Atlantic to Istanbul walk which, at a mere 4390 km (2473 miles), might be more suitable than the E2 if you're pushed for time. The British stretch starts at Anglesey, crosses Snowdonia and the Pennines and ends in Hull.

So the puny 110 or so miles of the Cleveland Way can act as a warm-up. By the time you get to Filey you will have done about 62 miles of the E2. Only 2968 to go.

Guisborough

The path opens out briefly to give an expansive view of the sea out past Guisborough and further out Redcar, Marske and then Teesside, the Tees and the coast of County Durham up almost as far as Sunderland on a good day.

The Cleveland Way is in fact not the path to the front but the one which disappears off to the right and on up to the top of the Nab. It's a good place for a brief stop, though, to watch the bustle of the towns below as they go about their daily business.

One thing about Guisborough – should you decide to call there – is that you will not go wanting for a pub. There are at least 12 on or near the main marketplace. The charter for the market was granted by Henry II in 1263.

The town is half encircled by the commercial spruce and larch plantations of the Forestry Commission.

The town has about 20,000 people, many of them working in Teesside. Its origins go back almost certainly to Saxon times but William the Conqueror gave it to Robert de Brus. If you think that sounds a bit like Robert the Bruce then you wouldn't be far wrong. The Scottish Bruce was a direct descendent through a series of Roberts and the "de" became "the" somewhere along the line. Guisborough has been called variously Chigesburg, Ghigesburgh, Ghigesborg Ghigesbore and Giseborne. Gisborough Priory isn't a misprint.

We've already passed the alum workings by Carlton in the Cleveland Hills, and we'll come to them again, particularly at Boulby Cliff, but it's worth mentioning here that Sir Thomas Chaloner, an Elizabethan soldier scholar and statesman, is supposed to have discovered and developed the first alum mines near Guisborough in 1595. Alum production at the time was the monopoly of the Pope and Chaloner apparently enticed some of the Italians over to sunny Guisborough to practice their art in Cleveland. The Pope excommunicated him, which is what he did to everybody else who tried to break the Papal monopoly, but it didn't seem to bother Thomas any more than it had bothered Henry VIII or Elizabeth I.

Guisborough from Highcliff Nab

143

Cleveland's Capital

On the road signs which signal the start of Guisborough it styles itself the "Ancient Capital of Cleveland".

The name Cleveland is a derivative of Cliff Land, and the Cleveland Way is aptly named, even though only about 13 miles of it from Slapewath to just outside Staithes is situated in the old Cleveland County. Once it emerges from the little dales out of Helmsley the walk is on escarpment edges for most of the way to Saltburn and is then one long cliff top walk for 50 miles until it reaches Filey. The cliffs carry on as the chalk cliffs from Filey, getting progressively lower as they go around Flamborough Head, finally petering out at Bridlington. From then on down things are, geologically and scenically, somewhat different.

Cleveland as a legal entity in an administrative sense only came into existence in 1974 from an agglomeration of the existing Teesside boroughs (mainly Middlesbrough and Stockton but also comprising Billingham, Thornaby, Eston, Redcar and other smaller towns and villages cobbled together under one name in 1967) and Hartlepool, itself a combination of ancient Hartlepool and the Victorian West Hartlepool. Cleveland, unloved as it was by many of the people who live there, survived until the reorganisation of 1996 when four new separate unitary authorities of Hartlepool, Stockton, Middlesbrough and Redcar & Cleveland were created.

The new authorities are all self-contained unitary structures with responsibilities for delivery of all local services, and for certain purposes they have been joined by Darlington. For ceremonial purposes the boroughs have reverted to their old counties – Middlesbrough and Redcar and Cleveland to North Yorkshire and Stockton and Hartlepool to Durham. It has created one anomaly – the parts of Stockton south of the Tees that used to be in Yorkshire and are now, ceremonially at least, in Durham.

Cleveland went from being the sum of the whole to a part of one constituent overnight. Guisborough is in Redcar and Cleveland and some of the council services have been moved there. Once again, Guisborough is, for a few things, the capital of Cleveland.

Guisborough from the escarpment above Guisborough Woods

145

Priory

Two miles off the Cleveland Way in Guisborough proper we have another pile of stones in the care of English Heritage. Henry again.

Gisborough Priory was the home of the Augustinian Canons – not an enclosed monastic order like the Cistercians or Carthusians, but a group who lived under a monastic code but supplied clergy to the local area.

Gisborough Priory is the second oldest religious institution we pass on the journey – the oldest settlement was at Whitby, although not necessarily in terms of what's left today.

Gisborough was founded by Robert de Brus probably between 1119 and 1124. Robert and the early de Brus family were buried here, including Robert de Brus IV of the Annandale branch of the family, grandfather to Robert the Bruce, victor at Bannockburn and King of Scotland.

Building the priory continued well into the thirteenth century. However in 1289 there was a disastrous fire, the cause of which was recorded by Walter of Hemingborough, a historian and subprior of Gisborough from 1302.

On the morning of May 16 1289, a plumber was working with two assistants on repairs to cracks in the lead of the south transept roof. In the middle of the morning he came down, leaving his two boys to put out the burning charcoal in the iron pans which he'd left on some dry timbers on the roof. The young lads didn't put out the fires properly and a gust of wind caught the pans, scattering the embers and re-lighting the charcoal. The fire took hold, burning the timbers and melting the lead which poured down from the roof into the church. The fire spread throughout the building destroying the roof completely and most of the church contents, including furniture, statues, vestments, relics, books and ornaments.

Although rebuilding started soon afterwards there were further problems caused by the Scots after they defeated Edward II at Bannockburn in 1314. The Scots were frequent visitors to these parts over the years, and they didn't come to admire the view or to walk the Cleveland Way. The work was probably not completed until the late 1300s and survived about 150 years.

The Cleveland Way is on top of the wooded hills above Gisborough Priory

Ruin

The demise of Gisborough Priory follows the usual predictable path.

Gisborough Priory was found to have a net annual value of £628 6s 8d which made it the fourth richest in Yorkshire after York, Fountains and Selby. The first wave of suppression in 1536 dissolved the establishments with annual income of less than £200, so Gisborough was granted a brief reprieve. The categorisation of the establishments by a financial criterion makes it quite obvious that the motivation for the destruction of so much architecture was not for religious reasons but so Henry could get his hands on their money.

In 1516 some 500 families in Guisborough were dependent on the Priory for their living and resentment of the new changes was widespread. The commissioners replaced the existing prior, James Cockerell, with Robert Pursglove who they thought would be more compliant. After the dissolution of Gisborough Priory on 8 April 1540 Pursglove was awarded an annual pension of £166 13s 4d – a huge sum of money in those days –and continued in the church as a bishop and archdeacon of Nottingham. He was deprived of these in 1559 after refusing to take the Oath of Supremacy to Elizabeth.

The suppression of the religious establishments resulted in a rebellion known as the Pilgrimage of Grace. It was of course doomed to failure. Pursglove kept clear of it but Cockerell, who by this time had retired to Lythe, got involved. He was executed at Tyburn.

The Priory was leased to Thomas Legh, a henchman of Henry's who had played a major part in the destruction of the monasteries and was then sold to Sir Thomas Chaloner in 1550. The cloisters and the nave of the church were cleared away to make way for formal gardens in 1709 by which time the cloister had been used as a sunken bowling green.

The Chaloner mansion – Old Gisborough Hall – was demolished in 1825 and his new house, Gisborough Hall was built in 1857. This building is now an hotel a half mile outside Guisborough on the way to the Cleveland Way.

Slapewath

Back to the track then, and just past Guisborough it emerges from the woodland where we left it to look at the priory. It turns into a rather incongruous concrete road which appears to go nowhere in particular. In fact it leads to Round Close Farm, but leading off it there are some strange side roads and gated entrances into the hillside.

It's a little eerie finding these locked gates in the middle of nowhere with no signs or signposts as to what they are or why they were made. They were, as it turns out, constructed during the second World War as an infrastructure for the local tank training grounds and gunnery ranges.

The path descends through the woodland from the escarpment above Guisborough to the busy A171 moor road to Whitby.

At the bottom of the hill is the row of houses known as Charltons, birthplace of Tom Leonard (later). The path crosses the road, turns towards Guisborough and makes its way towards the Fox and Hounds, the long awaited post-Osmotherley pub.

At this point the Cleveland Way intersects Cleveland Street, yet another waymarked path which purports to re-create the old monastic route between Guisborough Priory and Whitby Abbey. At the moment it goes as far as Loftus – a mile or so south of our cliff-top high point at Boulby Cliff and rather less than half way to Whitby.

The Cleveland Way climbs back up onto the high ground passing around a quarry, up a hill with a last view across to the moors, through a wood and then out onto arable farmland, now with clear views towards Teesside, Saltburn and the coast.

The view to the right on the picture opposite looks out to the cliffs east of Saltburn and we are approaching the end of the inland phase of the Cleveland Way – about half of the total length of the trail. From now on there are a pleasant variety of villages, shops and pubs interspersed with the odd town or two. And lots of stunning cliff scenery.

The path to Airy Hill Lane

Skelton

Skelton is a workaday village in the north Cleveland area. North Skelton was the site of the very last ironstone mine worked in what at one time was an extensive industry. The major production occurred between about 1850 and 1954. The seam of iron ore was up to 17ft thick and was mined at outcrops in the north west at Middlesbrough, Eston Nab and Ormesby and in the east near Staithes. The seam dips into a basin around Skelton and so deep mining was necessary to extract it. The ore was of considerably lower quality than the minerals available from Labrador, Sweden and Spain – in England typically 20% to 40% and at Skelton 30% as against the 60% from elsewhere. North Skelton was the last mine to close in 1964.

William the Conqueror gave 51 manors to Robert de Brus, 13 of them in Yorkshire. Robert was a great friend of David, Earl of Huntingdon, who, through marriage, inherited the throne of Scotland in 1124, and awarded his friend Robert de Brus the Lordship of Annandale in South West Scotland. David declared war on England and Robert found himself in the awkward position of having a foot in both camps. The action he took was to split his English and Scottish holdings, assigning his English estates to his eldest son Adam and the Scottish estates to his 14 year old son Robert, believing him too young to fight. It would appear that the genes were passed on along the line, because Robert took to the field with David at the Battle of the Standards where the Scots were trounced. It's quite easy to get confused from here on in because the famous King Robert the Bruce of Bannockburn was the seventh Lord Annandale and all six of his predecessors were also called Robert. But that's what makes the connection between the small mining town in Cleveland and the "Flower of Scotland" eulogised in Roy Williamson's song, now *de facto* Scotland's National Anthem.

Skelton Castle was founded by the first Lord of Annandale around 1140 and lasted until it was demolished by John Hall Stephenson in 1788, when the existing structure was built. At one time it was a bit of a literary centre having strong associations with Laurence Sterne, author of Tristram Shandy.

Skelton Castle is private property and is not open to the public.

Skelton Castle and the view up the County Durham coast over the Tees estuary

Skelton Beck to Saltburn

It is here that the Cleveland Way meets the first of the towns and villages of East Cleveland. It first passes into Skelton Green and then follows a steep descent into Skelton itself. Skelton High Street used to form part of the main A174 Guisborough to Whitby coast road but now it bypasses Skelton, North Skelton and Brotton. The Way through Skelton involves small town footpaths in a housing estate for a few hundred yards but once we pass under the new road we're back into woodland, dropping down to join Skelton Beck as it runs into Saltburn and the sea.

A footbridge takes the Cleveland Way under the big viaduct arches carrying the railway. This line is the old coast line which at one time connected Middlesbrough to Whitby. The line followed the existing Saltburn route but branched off to Loftus, Staithes and Whitby. It was closed after Dr Beeching's demolition job but reopened in 1972 after the discovery of large deposits of potassium chloride near Boulby resulted in the Cleveland Potash Mine being sunk to extract it. The railway enables large quantities of this mineral to be transported to the company's own deep water terminal at Teesmouth.

The path continues along the bottom of the woodland before rising up to meet the streets of Saltburn above the Valley Gardens. An impressive toll bridge was built to cross the ravine here, high above the stream, in 1869 (for pedestrians and horse-drawn carriages only). The bridge was named after the toll charge – the ha'penny bridge, and over the years it gradually gained notoriety for people jumping off into the valley below, doing themselves a fatal injury in the process. When it became apparent that, owing to its deterioration, it might actually kill people who didn't want to end their days, it was declared unsafe and spectacularly demolished with a controlled explosion in 1974. In the summer months a miniature railway runs from a little station by the beck at the bottom of the valley alongside the stream to the Italian Gardens, and a pleasant little ride it is.

Saltburn marks a sensible break in the walk. There are pubs, cafes and restaurants, buses and a railway connection to Middlesbrough. It also marks roughly the half way point in the Cleveland Way. From now until Filey Brigg the walk is entirely along cliff tops, punctuated by Nabs, Wykes and villages.

Skelton Beck underneath the Mineral line viaduct

Pier

Saltburn is an old seaside village which made merry by smuggling just about anything worthwhile until the industrialist Henry Pease decided that the region needed a Brighton of the north for genteel people (no riff-raff) to enjoy the sea air. There are about 5 miles of sands along past Redcar towards the Tees and there is almost a quarter of a mile of beach out to sea at low tide. And so it came to pass that he extended the Stockton and Darlington Railway to Saltburn, finally reaching its destination on 17 August 1861.

The Zetland Hotel was built (the big creamy coloured brick building which is now a complex of apartments), the ha'penny toll bridge and the pier in 1869. At one time the pier was 1400 feet long with a landing stage for steamers at the end. The first of its major problems occurred in 1874 and 1875 when violent storms wrecked the landing stage and a part of the main structure was lost to storms. The pier re-opened in 1877 at 1250 ft in length, but there was more storm damage in 1900 and a collision with the *Ovenberg* in 1924. The pier was closed off to the public at the start of the second World War and re-opened in 1952. Not for long.

A severe gale the next year twisted the whole structure and repairs took five years. No sooner had it reopened (again) when two piles were lost and yet again in 1961 twenty piles were twisted. In 1971, 1973 and 1974 further piles were lost and as plans were being made for emergency repairs another storm washed away the pier head. The council had had enough and applied to have the structure demolished. Against the odds it survived an enquiry and only the last thirteen trestles were destroyed. It opened again on 29th June 1978, truncated to 681ft. Unsurprisingly it is the only amusement pier on the North East Coast.

The Cliff Lifts in the picture date from about the time of the pier and are powered by characteristic Victorian ingenuity.

Water is pumped up the cliff and into a tank on the car at the top. Slowly a brake is released and the extra weight lowers one car while pulling the bottom one up by a system of cables and pulleys. When the car reaches the bottom the water is emptied. Simple.

Saltburn – the remains of the pier and the cliff lift

157

Smugglers

In the eighteenth century Saltburn was a little fishing backwater, well away from the big towns, of concern to no-one in particular other than the people who lived, worked and died here.

Not quite. Take a look around you and you will see ideal smuggling country – a small, isolated community, a small beach between two high cliffs which could give plenty of warning both ways of approaching vessels. The fishermen had another, far more lucrative trade. Tea, coffee, brandy, gin, textiles and other necessities were highly taxed and the evasion of the duty a lucrative business.

Saltburn's most famous smuggler was John Andrew, a Scotsman, who became landlord of the Ship Inn in about 1780. The Ship is the white building right centre of the picture beyond the car park at the bottom of the cliff. He had attained the "Sublime degree of Master Mason", was a pillar of society, first Master of Cleveland Hounds and he had his own lugger – the Morgan Rutter. His home – the White House, was reputedly linked to the Ship Inn by a tunnel.

The surrounding communities of Marske and Cotham were notorious and it seems that smuggling was very much a local industry because it was carried out in broad daylight. They weren't, of course, the romantic lovable rogues of modern perception. They were vicious and violent men, quite prepared to enter battle and to injure and kill if required.

After many near misses John Andrew was finally arrested in Hornsea on the Holderness Coast in 1827. He was imprisoned for two years at York and died, aged 74, in 1835.

The end of the Napoleonic Wars had freed up Royal Navy ships to patrol the coast and this, together with a reduction of taxes, made the smuggling trade less profitable and more risky.

There is a smugglers museum by the Ship Inn if you want to find out more about this particular activity. As an enterprise it was very common along the villages in the next section of the walk.

Cliffs

You are about to embark on the clifftop walk which comprises about half of the 110 miles of the Cleveland Way. It is very different from the first half for lots of reasons. The sea is now a constant companion, sometimes only one giant step to the left (and several hundreds of feet down). We pass through many villages and towns, some working and some now only populated at weekends and when the weather's nice.

The stretch between Saltburn and Scalby Ness, just north of Scarborough, has been given the status of "Heritage Coast" by the Countryside Agency. Although this does not confer any statutory rights or obligations it is a formal recognition that this coastline is worthy of particular care and attention. Much of the 35 miles of the Heritage Coast lies within the North York Moors National Park and therefore already has protection. The section of the coast from just south of Filey down past Flamborough Head is now the "Flamborough Headland Heritage Coast" leaving the stretch between Scarborough and Filey as the only non-urbanised part of the Yorkshire coast between Saltburn and Bridlington without Heritage Coast status.

Past the Ship Inn and up to the top of the cliffs and here we are with the sea on the left and the path next to the drop. The walk for the next 50 plus miles is largely made of the boulder clays which you see here.

The coastal section of the Cleveland Way is probably overall the busiest. It can be exhilarating, attractive and exciting with the open sea to the east and the superb vistas along the cliffs all the way down to the end of the trail.

It does have its moments though, for people like me who get a bit wobbly with heights. It's wide enough all the way, but it's worth repeating the National Trail Guide's "Cleveland Way" advice to take care, especially in wet and windy weather. This, as you will see, is eminently sensible, but you'd be surprised, as I can testify personally....

The first time I ever walked along part of this coastal path was before the Cleveland Way was born and I was 14 years old, in a school party that set off to walk from Staithes to Whitby. We got as far as Runswick Bay. The rain was torrential, helped along by a howling westerly gale. It was interesting.

Atop Huntcliff and fifty miles of cliff walking ahead

Sculpture

One advantage of a cliff path such as this is that it's impossible to take a wrong turning. Travelling north to south, most of the route to the right is fenced off and all of it to the left is down. All the way to the sea.

The clifftop path approaches Warsett Hill, a mound which rises about 120 feet above the clifftop level. Our path steers cliffside of the Boulby Potash mineral railway which forms a loop around the hill. If you should encounter one of the trains here the experience is interesting. Once you feel the vibration of the ground underneath your feet you will marvel that the whole cliff didn't collapse years ago.

There are three iron sculptures by the wayside here, the most striking being the 7 foot diameter circle which represents a new type of pit prop relating to iron stone mining. On this are hung ten sculpted three dimensional images relating to the work and history of the area.

A horse (for the Cleveland Bay horse)

A starfish (for the shore)

A pigeon (for the fanciers in Skinningrove)

A cat (in the 1300s cats were hunted here – hence Hunt Cliff. Allegedly.)

A merman (one of these creatures was reputedly washed up on Skinningrove beach in 1607)

A nautilus/belemnite (for fossils – loads of them later)

A piece of protoplasm (basic to life – only a madman or a genius would attempt to sculpt a piece of protoplasm)

Thor's hammer (relating to working metal/blacksmiths not to mention the Norse god of thunder)

A ring (Lifebelt)

A mermaid's purse (common to the seashore)

Richard Farrington (the sculptor in question) made them as a part of the "Skelton and Brotton New Milestones Project". The sculpture was completed in 1990.

The Romans had a signal station on Hunt Cliff and it would appear that the coastal footpath was used by the Iron Age peoples three hundred years before that, as tumuli nearby on Warsett Hill (on the other side of the railway line) would seem to indicate.

One of the iron sculptures alongside the clifftop mineral line to Boulby Mine

Shinkansen

Our national trail meanders along its way with green fields to the right until we come to Skinningrove. The first we see of it is the derelict stone pier jutting forlornly out into the North Sea with the marvellous Cattersty Sands beach leading into the village itself. The hulking Boulby Cliff looms ominously in the background.

I just thought I'd mention in passing that I always think that Boulby Cliff looks a bit like the motor units of the trains that run on the Shinkansen – the Japanese Bullet Train – sideways on. Not that it's of any great relevance, I just offer the observation *en passant,* and if it's confirmation you want then there's now one in the National Railway Museum in York.

There are claims that Boulby provides the final resting place for Beowulf, the Anglo Saxon hero of (very) early English Literature. The description given in the poem speaks of a big headland sounding very much like a description of Boulby Cliff and it doesn't take a huge leap of faith to imagine the Scandinavianisation of what would have been Beowulf-by to Boulby.

The line on the cliff is what's left of the coastal Middlesbrough to Whitby passenger route, discarded along with most other rural railways by Dr. Beeching. It was completed in 1867 and the primary driving force in its construction was the need to transport East Cleveland ironstone from the mines to the blast furnaces of rapidly expanding Middlesbrough. The line was reopened in 1967 to service the Potash mine – more of which later.

Before the ironstone was systematically mined, local people used to collect ironsone nodules that used to fall from the iron bearing layers in the cliffs as coastal erosion took its toll (then as now). As a cottage industry it had much to recommend it but the quality was dubious and the availability depended much on the weather and the tides. It isn't totally out of the question that some of the wily locals used to beef up their catch with some extra rocks which might not have been exactly what the furnaces were looking for.

This particular local industry came to an end in 1847 with the opening of the first ironstone mine in Skinningrove.

Skinningrove Pier

This rather sad wreck is what remains of Skinningrove Pier. It is now sealed off part way along. It wasn't always like this – the one and only time I tried sea fishing was off the end of this construction, aided and abetted by my father-in-law. I caught one small crab and a shoe.

Skinningrove is an old ironstone mining village with a steel works on the top of the cliff. Remarkably, given the rationalisation and closures elsewhere in the industry, the small Skinningrove steel works is still there although the workforce has been reduced from 3500 in 1958 to 350 at the end of 2004.

Unlike some of the small villages which occupy the gaps in the cliffs along the Cleveland Way, Skinningrove is still a living community, in sharp contrast to other places which are now home to few other than second homers and weekenders.

It is also unique along the Way in that it is home to the only dune system along this part of the coast. Over 220 varieties of plants have been recorded along the stretch of coast between Saltburn and Skinningrove and meadows have recently been created above Skinningrove from derelict land no longer used by the steel works. Species were introduced into these meadows that aren't normally found in the area, including yellow chamomile, corncockle, fodder burnet, cornflour, sainfoin, crimson clover, common bird's foot trefoil and tufted vetch. These last two attracted a large number of butterflies and the six spot burnet moth.

Large quantities of slag were tipped over Skinningrove cliffs by the mining industry and this is clearly visible on the cliff face as you approach the pier. This has been colonised by several plants including a number of orchids, one of which is the particularly beautiful pyramidal orchid *(Anacamptis pyramidalis)*.

The last ironstone mine in Skinningrove closed in 1958 and evidence of the minewater's presence is visible as you cross Skinningrove Beck.

Tom Leonard

This is Skinningrove Beach when the days are at their longest. Whether the future will bring change to this community time will only tell. The beach, the cliffs and the dunes are a far cry from the heaving pleasure beaches of the big resorts but maybe, one day, change will come. Most of the weekend-cottage villages along the coast to the south of here were once fishing communities – Skinningrove mutated from fishing to steel and its industrial past has given it a different character to Staithes, Runswick Bay and Robin Hood's Bay, but its setting and easy accessibility just off the main road must be a factor in where its future lies.

Skinningrove's mining history, and that of the many ironstone mining settlements around these parts, is commemorated in the Cleveland Ironstone Mining Museum (formerly the Tom Leonard Mining Museum).

The Museum is located on the site of Loftus Mine in Skinningrove, which was the first ironstone mine to open in Cleveland. At its peak the ironstone mining industry supported some 82 (some sources say 83) mines, and the annual production peaked at nearly 7 million tons.

The Cleveland ironstone seam was discovered at Skinningrove in 1847 when one Samuel Frederick Okey was examining ironstone on the beach and Anthony Lax Maynard, a local landowner, commented on the same colour stone that he'd noticed further up the valley. Okey went for a look and discovered the valuable seam which was worked for just over 110 years.

The ironstone production started at the Loftus Ironstone Mine in Skinningrove on 7th August 1848 and closed on 26th September 1958.

As you asked, Tom Leonard was a newspaper reporter for the Middlesbrough Evening Gazette. He was born in 1922 at Charltons, the small group of houses we passed through coming down from the moors just before Slapewath. He served in the RAF and became a reporter when he returned to civilian life. He had wanted to set up a museum devoted to the ironstone miners and his wife, family and friends got it organised in his memory.

Zeppelins

During the U Boat campaigns of 1914 at the start of the First World War, Skinningrove Steel Works added two steel furnaces and a mixer to the plant and doubled the size of its coke-oven installations in order to manufacture shell steel.

The by-products of these ovens were used to make high explosives and in Skinningrove they did it the dangerous way.

In 1915 the Ministry of Munitions encouraged the manufacture of TNT by the "one stage" method. Two special buildings were built on the western cliffs to dissipate the shock waves in the event of an explosion during manufacture. This was done with the noble intention of inflicting less damage to the people of Carlin How. Much to their undoubted relief, in 1916 they reverted to the far safer "two stage process". During that time two and a half million pounds of high explosive was manufactured at Skinningrove. Research was also carried out into the manufacture of poison gas from ethylene which was a by-product from the manufacture of coke from coal in the coke ovens.

With the steel, high explosives and poison gas, it's little wonder that Skinningrove should attract the attention of the German High Command.

One September night in 1916 three Zeppelins – 804 feet long and 135 feet in diameter at their widest point – approached Skinningrove and dropped over one hundred bombs on the works. As the German High Fleet had bombarded Scarborough, Whitby and Hartlepool a few months earlier, the people of Skinningrove had high expectations of a visitation of this nature and had taken the precaution of arranging hiding places in the hedgerows and in the mineworkings.

Some of the bombs were incendiaries, and these landed on the roof of the benzol house which contained a stockpile of highly inflammable materials.

Surprisingly, given the nature of the works and its products, the only serious damage was sustained by the Steel Plant Offices and there were no reports of any casualties.

Coble and sheds by Skinningrove beach

Boulby

The Cleveland Way passes through Skinningrove and crosses Kilton Beck, then up and along the clifftop path which leads to the highest point on the coastline of Eastern England. Boulby Cliff.

The climb up to the top of the cliff isn't done in one giant step but progresses sensibly in stages along the clifftop path and then inland through farmland. Likewise, much of Boulby Cliff doesn't fall in one steep drop to the sea but is shelved to a greater or lesser extent. In part this is due to the workings of the alum industry, which flourished on the side of this cliff, but there is at least one section, just behind Boulby Barns Farm, where the true height of the Cleveland Way above the North Sea is quite straightforwardly apparent. This is at the cliff's highest point where walkers on the path get a grand view over the edge to the water and rocks 660 feet below.

Boulby is an interesting place, having in the past had associations with ironstone, jet and alum and is now, somewhat surprisingly, playing host to an experiment which places it at the forefront of theoretical physics, cosmology and the search for the meaning of the universe. A small contribution in the grand scheme of things, but not many places along the Cleveland Way can lay claim to be involved in the quest for an answer to the ultimate question the universe has to pose.

The oldest surface rocks hereabout belong to the Lower Jurassic period of about 200 million years ago when the area was under sea water and was home to the life forms now fossilised on the beaches near Runswick Bay and Robin Hood's Bay.

The Middle Jurassic, about 170 million years ago, saw the sea levels falling and the area was river channels and swamps.

The Upper Jurassic was once again shallow ocean and the microscopic life forms which lived here left their calcium-based skeletons to form the limestones along the Tabular Hills and the part of the Cleveland Way along Sutton Bank.

Alum

Alum used to be a valuable material. Until the eighteenth century the science of chemistry was unknown and alchemy held sway, with its aim of turning base metal into gold. Even Isaac Newton, whose mathematics and physics quite literally changed the world, dabbled in alchemy. When the chemists got hold of coal they made all sorts of things out of it including aniline dyes, which reduced the importance of alum.

Alum was much prized for several reasons, one of the principal uses being as a fixative for dyes. The natural dyestuffs of the alchemy era were "fixed" to the natural fibres by treating the fibres with alum. This chemical has been used since before 2000BC although the science behind it has been understood for less than 200 years.

If fibres are treated with natural dyes obtained (mainly) by boiling up plants, or beetles (for cochineal) then when they are washed the dye leeches out and eventually disappears. To prevent this happening the textiles are first boiled up with a mordant or fixative, which, when coloured, binds the dye to the fibre and makes it fast. One of the most important mordants is alum. Alum was the key to the successful colouring of wool and silk.

Until the middle of the fifteenth century the sole source was Asia Minor and the main trading was done with the Italian states. When Constantinople fell to the Muslims in 1543 the pope objected to the trade and alternative sources were sought. One John di Castro, a cloth dyer who had worked in Constantinople, was chased back to Italy, where he discovered an alum rock. He was rewarded by the pope who set up alum works at Tolfa (still there today) and established a commercial monopoly throughout the non-islamic world. For anyone attempting to break the monopoly the pope had a simple solution. They were excommunicated. At that time the threat wasn't only the promise of eternal damnation, it had a great many practical consequences. As monopolists do, the pope pushed the price as high as he could get away with. Sir Thomas Chaloner founded the first alum works in this country near Guisborough. It is said that he recognised a discolouration in tree foliage that was associated with the presence in the ground of aluminium compounds.

175

Chemistry

Pure alum is a white crystal that looks a bit like sugar. It is a "complex salt" meaning that there is a negatively charged sulphate constituent with two different positively charged constituents instead of the one which is found in simple salts. All alums have aluminium as one of their positives and the two that were manufactured here had either potassium or ammonium as the other.

The preparation of alum from the crude shales was essentially a six-stage process which took a year or more from start to finish.

Firstly the shale was mined in the traditional manner of early industrial Britain – by men with pickaxes paid by the amount they could dig. They would tip the shale onto a pile of brushwood which was set alight. Coal and more shale was added until the heap was getting on for a hundred feet high. It was left to burn for about a year.

The chemistry starts here. The shales contained aluminium silicates and iron pyrites – a sulphide. The burning of the coal created sulphurous gases which were sealed into the heap and reacted with the aluminium there to form crude aluminium sulphate.

The heap became more porous and eventually shrunk to about half its original size. When it was opened up the pile had changed colour from grey to pink.

This crude product was then tipped into tanks where water was added and left to dissolve the alum over several days. The liquid containing the salts was passed from tank to tank and the impurities left were dug out and discarded.

The liquor was then clarified by boiling for 24 hours and passed to a settling tank. The iron silicates fell to the bottom and the clear liquid was treated with either kelp (for potassium alum) or stale human urine (for ammonium alum) and sent to the cooling house, where the crude alum dropped out of solution as it cooled.

The final stage in the process was to dig out the crude alum, dissolve it again in boiling water and allow it to cool for eight days after which the alum had crystallised out. The remaining liquid, which was of course still saturated with the alum salt in solution, was run off, collected and returned to the third stage of the manufacturing process.

After a further eight days the crystalline alum was ready.

Staithes from Boulby Cliff

Dark Matter

The cliffs were an ideal place for alum works because the transfer of the material from one stage to the next was effected by the simple expedient of tipping it further down the cliff until it reached the final purification stages at the bottom. Gravity to the rescue. Which brings us neatly to the subject of Dark Matter.

Most of the universe is missing – 96% of it to be precise (figure is the latest one as of January 2004). Cosmologists know this because their calculations show that the universe we see has too much gravity. The 100 billion stars in 100 billion galaxies shouldn't be able to hold the universe together as it is observed. So there must be something out there which we can't see and can't measure but accounts for 96% of all the gravitational effects which we can see and can measure.

One solution which pops out of the myriad equations theoretical physicists use to model the universe proposes what they have called "wimps" or weakly interacting massive particles. These strange creatures, although they have mass, are missing other characteristics of matter which means that we can't detect them reliably by the normal means we use for protons and electrons, usually involving some form of electromagnetic interaction. However, according to the theoretical physicists, occasionally we should be able to detect a statistically very small number of interactions with normal matter under certain specific circumstances. Unfortunately, these are so rare and difficult to detect that they, in theory remember, get lost in the noise of the cosmic and terrestrial background radiation which surrounds us on all sides.

The solution is to put the experiment deep underground. This is as deep as it gets in Europe. The Boulby potash mine (extracting that potassium chloride laid down during the evaporation of the salt lake 300 million years ago) is the deepest mine in Europe at about 4000 ft. The scientists looking for dark matter have set up their detectors at the bottom of the mine. Results calculated at the end of 2003 suggest that only 23% of the missing 96% is dark matter, the other 73% is dark energy. Nobody has a clue what this is about, but everything we see is made up of it, including us.

179

Uncertainty

"The Universe is not only queerer than we suppose, it's queerer than we can suppose" said the British scientist JBS Haldane. Too right. Dark Energy is supposed to contribute 73% of the mass of the known universe – although how it's known when we don't know what 96% of the universe is made of I don't know – and the effect this Dark Energy has is apparently to push the furthest known galaxies away from us at ever increasing speeds. Not only this but we are told by some cosmologists that the dimensions we see in every day life (up and down, back and front, left and right and time) are only four of twelve. Or thirteen. Or twenty six. And the Heisenberg Uncertainty Principle has been telling us since the 1930s that we cannot be certain of anything we can measure because the act of measuring interferes with the measurement. Once thought to be of esoteric relevance to subatomic particles this has now become an important consideration in the design of microelectronic circuits and may well be the basis of a whole new breed of supercomputers – the quantum machines which can compute all the solutions to a problem at the same time – provided you don't watch what they're doing.

When I was a student the students' paper carried a spoof story. "A theoretical physicist yesterday fell down the hole at the centre of a toroidal universe. His colleagues are now trying to find out if this was possible." At least at the time I thought it was a spoof. Now I'm not so sure.

Carl Sagan wrote a book called Pale Blue Dot – a reference to the significance of planet earth as seen from just outside the solar system. Pale Blue Dot would appear to exaggerate its importance.

So that's what's going on almost a mile beneath your feet as you descend Boulby Cliff with its old eyesore of alum workings and its new eyesore of the smoking stacks of the potash mine. Recently the mine owners applied for permission for expansion of the workings to include salt (as in sodium chloride or common salt) extraction. It will extend the lifetime of the mine by at least twenty five years. Good news in lots of respects but it is a bit of a mess.

But maybe its Dark Matter experiment might help provide us with a clue as to what we're made of.

The North Sea Trail

Nortrail – The North Sea Trail – is an international project linking the communities that have coasts on the North Sea. From the north and clockwise it involves many authorities and agencies from Norway, Sweden, Denmark, Germany, the Netherlands, England and Scotland.

The coastal trails implicit in the title are only one component of the whole concept, albeit a very important component and the physical thread by which all the other parts are connected.

The project is categorised in four themes:

Nortrail is to:

Create a Pathways Network
Create a Heritage Network
Develop an Accommodation Network
and
Develop a Pathway to Knowledge

So as well as funding the walking route, the Nortrail project is helping to pay to develop links with the natural and cultural heritage sites along the coastlines of the North Sea countries. This will ultimately improve access to these important heritage sites for everybody.

Not only that, the Nortrail funding is allowing a fresh interpretation of the coast by helping to produce new guides, and the evidence for its success is in your hands right now. You are reading one of them.

The North York Moors National Park has contributed to the Nortrail project with the coastal section of the Cleveland Way.

The other British sections include Moray & Nairn, the Aberdeenshire Coast, the Fife Coast, East Lothian and the Northumberland Coast. As an aside, I can claim some affinity with the Fife Coast section because I lived there for four years when I was a student at St. Andrews University. North Sea Trailers will be sampling the delights of St. Andrews, Crail, Anstruther and Pittenweem.

So not only are you walking the Cleveland Way and part of the E2 long distance path, you've also bagged a bit of the North Sea Trail.

High Tide at Staithes with the Cleveland Way section of the North Sea Trail on the cliff tops

183

Staithes

Staithes as it now is isn't a particularly old place. Most of the village dates from the seventeenth century, and was based mainly on the three industries of this coastline: fishing, mining and smuggling, and not necessarily in that order.

The young James Cook arrived in Staithes in 1744 aged 16 to be apprenticed to William Sanderson, a haberdasher and general storekeeper. The likely connection is through Thomas Skottowe, James Cook senior's employer at Aireyholme Farm who was also a Justice of the Peace. He would have attended sessions in Guisborough. Sanderson, in addition to his shopkeeping, acted as Constable in the district. The young James would have slept under the counter and worked long hours. He didn't like it. Staithes seems to have given him the seagoing bug, and so, after eighteen months, when it became apparent to Sanderson that his charge was unhappy as a grocer, he used his connections to get James into the employment of the Walker family in Whitby.

James' sister Christiana married a Staithes fisherman surnamed Cocker. Her father, James senior, moved to Staithes and lived with them.

There is a new Staithes at the top of the short but steep road out of the village. The old railway station buildings still stand next to the Captain Cook Hotel and you can still see the stone structure which anchored the impressive iron viaduct which used to carry the line high across Roxby Beck. It was demolished in 1960 after the coastal clifftop railway to Whitby was closed. In order to add substance to the hollow steel structure the supports were filled with concrete. They can still be seen in the ravine.

This picture is of the main street in Staithes down at the bottom. Probably the best known pub in the village is the Cod and Lobster, perched on the sea wall, and famous for being trashed by storms, the latest occasion being in 1952, after which a substantial rebuild was necessary.

William Sanderson's shop was dismantled after a storm in 1812 and the materials were used to build the existing buildings in Church Street which now has a plaque on it commemorating "Captain Cook's Cottage". It isn't and it wasn't.

Staithes – the Royal George pub

Sandstone

Much of the building work in Staithes which was carried out in the nineteenth century was done using sandstone. Large quantities of good quality sandstone had become exposed on Boulby Cliff during the extensive excavations for alum shale. Three Methodist chapels were built around this period – the Congregational in 1821-22, the Wesleyan in 1865-66 and the Primitive Methodist in 1879-80. They were built back from the sea at the bottom of the hill. The Congregational is the one with the word "BETHEL" over the door. Nicholas Pevsner described it as "Egyptian" lettering.

In his book "STAITHES – Chapters from the history of a seafaring town" by John Howard (ISBN 0 9539005 0 9) I find that one Joseph Thurlow of Boulby was a trustee of the Wesleyan chapel and Levi Thurlow of Boulby Barns Farm was responsible for the dressing of the stone. Some local farmers provided the transport with their horses and carts which supplied them with additional income. One of these farmers was a Matthew Codling of Cowbar Farm. He addressed his bill to "Ranter Chapel, Staithes". Ranter was, shall we say, not the word the Wesleyans used to describe themselves. It was changed by the minister to "Primitive Methodist Chapel".

I mention this not just because of its background to the history of Staithes and one or two of its ancient inhabitants but because there is a personal interest. Matthew Codling is related to my family through my wife whose maiden name is Codling. Her grandmother was a Thurlow from Boulby Barns farm. Her father, my father-in-law, tells tales of visits to the farm when they used to climb down Boulby cliff to play football amongst the alum spoil heaps.

Staithes saw a naval engagement during the Napoleonic Wars. On June 12th 1804 the *Princess Augusta*, a Naval Cutter patrolling the stretch of sea off Staithes engaged a French privateer which had tried to force her to surrender. The cutter was heavily outgunned but the twenty six Sea Fencibles from Staithes (a sort of inshore Home Guard) got into their cobles and chased the Frenchman. For their part in the action three of them received three shillings and sixpence each, the rest two shillings.

Staithes slipway and Cowbar Nab

Fish and Smuggling

The Staithes fishing fleet is now reduced to a few cobles which ply for crabs and lobsters. Until the early part of the twentieth century things were very different. At its peak the fleet numbered some 300 vessels.

For some of the fishermen the income they earned from their legitimate business was supplemented by smuggling. Although this may seem a romantic notion to us nowadays, then, as now, organised crime isn't far below the surface.

It's quite likely that the big London smuggling gangs would have people working for them as far as Staithes. They hired hit men to kill for them. A murder in Staithes in October 1775 of a young man, Thomas Wastell, may well have been such an event. He was stabbed to death by a man known as James Rice or "Dutch Michael" from near Flushing in the Netherlands whose real surname was Rijks. Thomas was from a seafaring family and had become involved in smuggling. He appears to have talked too much and was stabbed outside William Andrews' cobbler's shop. The murder doesn't appear to have had any other motive, and Rice / Rijks' behaviour afterwards, when instead of running away swam out to sea, indicated that he may have been expecting to be met by a cutter to spirit him away.

This didn't happen and Rice was arrested. During his imprisonment his sanity was questioned because even in those days they didn't execute the mentally ill.

James Rice / Michael Rijks was eventually found to be sane and was executed on December 19th 1779 at the old gallows without Micklegate in York.

This wasn't the only death in Staithes which had smuggling connections although it is probably the only one which was perpetrated by organised gangs from outside the area. In 1769 one John Carr was killed from a shot fired from a naval vessel at the smuggling cutter he was manning and in 1776 Thomas Casseldine, a young Dragoon Guardsman, was bludgeoned to death by a sawn-off coble mast.

The slipway at Staithes and the harbour walls

Staithes Artists

Staithes is still a centre for artists and photographers. Visiting it, it isn't difficult to see why, with the narrow twisting alleys running behind the cobbled streets clinging to the cliff and almost tumbling into the sea, the small natural harbour and the precipitous cliffs with their gulls, fulmars and kittiwakes nesting on the narrow ledges.

The Staithes Group of artists was a formal group of painters who were encouraged to set up exhibitions by Dame Ethel Walker RA who lived in Scarborough. Their first annual exhibition was in 1901. By this time the fishing industry had collapsed and there was real poverty here. The coming of the railway in 1875 had opened up the village to the new breed of Victorian tourists from the big towns. The artists had followed and although a few of them had been summer visitors after 1890 a group of them had begun a movement to live here all year round. Earnest Dade, JR Bagshawe Rowland Hill and, probably most famously, Dame Laura Knight were one time members of the group which included many others. Jean and Peter Ecclestone's book (see next page) gives potted biographies of thirty of them but the definitive work of the Staithes Group was published by Dr Peter Phillips.

The 1914-18 war was one of the main factors which brought an end to the group with some members joining the armed forces. Others moved away to take up work in other areas, most famously to Newlyn where they founded the eponymous group.

Rowland Hill (a distant relation of the man who gave us the Penny Post) stayed on for the rest of his life, living a couple of miles down the Whitby road at Ellerby. He died in 1952 and is buried at Ugthorpe.

There is still an art group here and its activities are advertised in the windows of shops and houses. The post office and shops abound in paintings and photographs drawn, painted and pictured in oils, water colours, acrylics, charcoal, pencil and who knows what media.

The remains of the viaduct which carried the railway along the cliffs can be seen from here. I was a young child on holiday at Staithes when it was demolished in August 1960.

Seaton

The Cleveland Way passes through Staithes and up the lane past "Captain Cook's Cottage", by Cliff Farm and back onto the cliff top edge.

The path out of Staithes lies nearby the now vanished village of Seaton. Or Seton.

It dates back pre-conquest and was probably a Saxon settlement which suffered as much as anywhere else along this stretch of coastline at the hands of the Viking invaders.

For some reason Seaton was spared the genocide which William the Conqueror inflicted on the rest of Yorkshire. There were only eleven other places whose value in 1090 was the same as it was before the conquest. I quote from Jean and Peter Ecclestone's excellent book "A History and Geology of Staithes"....

"The destruction was deliberate, methodical, terrifying. Agricultural workers were slaughtered, crops burned, villages flattened, animals killed, ploughs and tools smashed, and, worst of all, the seed corn for the next year's food supply was purposely turned to ashes."

The next few pages will draw on this publication. If it's out of print (it's not always available) and you wish to influence the authors into getting another edition printed then pop into the post office at the bottom of the road into the village and have a word. They run it.

At the time Seaton was held by a man who is presumed to be a Saxon and whose name was Uhtred. For whatever reason he appears to have survived the slaughter with his land more or less intact when virtually the whole of the rest of Yorkshire was butchered or fled into slavery in Scotland or the midlands.

There used to be a Saxon church hereabouts but there is now no visible trace. It doesn't get a mention in the Domesday record.

Under the Norman feudal system the king was at the top of the heap. Under him were the first tier knights holding large swathes of land, who sublet it down the line. Below the king in this area were the Lords of Cleveland. These were the de Brus family.

The path nears the cliff edge near Beacon Hill on the approach to Port Mulgrave

Scotland

Herewith a potted history of the involvement of the local gentry on both sides in the machinations which culminated at the battle of Bannockburn in 1314.

King Robert the Bruce was a descendent of the de Brus family, William the Conqueror's Lords of Cleveland. Sir Christopher de Seaton was lord of the manor hereabouts and a friend of Robert's through the Cleveland connection.

The rivalries between the English and Scottish kings had led to wars and battles more or less since the Conquest. Alexander of Scotland had died in 1286, his heir being the 12-year-old Maid of Norway, who Edward I had had betrothed to his son, the Prince of Wales, the plan being to get his hands on the Scottish crown. It unravelled when the Maid died in a storm on the way to Scotland, but Edward wangled himself into a position where he would nominate the Scottish king. The two main contenders were Robert de Brus and John Balliol. Balliol won but was weak and abdicated. In 1297 the Scots middle classes rebelled under William Wallace. In 1305 Wallace was captured and executed, leaving chaos in the north.

Robert the Bruce and John "The Red" Comyn had struck up a bond but they fell out at Dumfries in 1305 where Robert attacked Comyn whose uncle, also a Robert, attacked the Bruce. Sir Christopher Seaton was with the Bruce and he killed Comyn's uncle – Comyn himself being finished off by two other of Bruce's associates. Robert the Bruce was crowned King of Scotland in 1306 and the local squire, Christopher de Seaton, was in attendance.

Edward I was less than happy and sent an army to meet the Scots. At the battle of Methven in 1306 the Scots were beaten and on Edward's instructions the Chivalric code was abandoned and no mercy was shown. Christopher Seaton was hung, drawn and quartered at Dumfries having been captured at Loch Doon castle. Sir Edmund de Mauley became the new lord of Seaton. He fought on the English side at the battle of Bannockburn in 1314 when Robert the Bruce got his own back. Edmund drowned in the burn. His home had been Mulgrave Castle.

Port Mulgrave

This bay with its now almost vanished harbour was never a fishing port nor an alum or jet mining site. What remains of the ruins of the harbour here is a legacy of the ironstone workings.

There was an ironstone seam east of Staithes which was worked in the 1850s. To ship this out, a wooden jetty was built at the bottom of Rosedale cliff, which became Port Mulgrave. These workings were bought by Charles Palmer in 1862 although the beach workings around Staithes had been owned by him since 1854. Palmer's industrial empire was huge and included coal and ironstone mining and transport, iron manufacture and shipbuilding on the Tyne at Jarrow. In 1865 he bought the Grinkle estate (a couple of miles inland from Boulby Cliff) and in 1869 he acquired Seaton. An ironstone seam had been discovered at Grinkle and a mine opened which operated until 1921 and then again briefly between 1927 and 1930.

A narrow gauge railway was built from Grinkle mine (not far from the present Boulby Potash complex) to bring the ore to Port Mulgrave. The waggons arrived at the port through a tunnel, the entrance to which is still visible, now sealed, part way up the cliff.

The jetties have been left to the mercies of the sea. My father-in-law used to own a coble with his brother from which he used to go fishing. He gave up when his equipment, on the shore, was vandalised. The decline in the condition of the piers over the past years has been dramatic. Twenty five years ago it was recognisable as a dilapidated harbour. Now it is a pile of stones.

Charles Palmer used his Grinkle estate as a country retreat and rebuilt Grinkle Hall in 1882. It is now the Grinkle Park Hotel. High on the sandstone walls there is a wyvern motif which was a characteristic emblem of the Templars, who may have counted among their number the unfortunate Christopher de Seaton. He was instrumental in the installation of major improvements in street lighting, water supply and sanitation to Staithes and endowed a school at Easington. He was liberal MP for North Durham from 1874 until his death in 1907. In October 1871 he accompanied Prime Minister Gladstone on a visit to Staithes.

What's left of the harbour at Port Mulgrave

Runswick

The steep metalled road down to Runswick Bay is on the right before the public car park. I always enjoy taking visitors here in a car – the road down is steep (25% all the way) and it feels like you're driving off the top of the world.

The Cleveland Way passes between the Cliffemount and the clifftop car park down the old road into Runswick Bay village. This is still metalled (after a fashion – it was once the main route down and gradients exceeded 33%) but vegetation has narrowed it to the point where you begin to wonder how anybody managed to ever get motor vehicles up and down, particularly if there was one on the way up and one going down. The Cleveland Way path is marked off here but in my own humble opinion there is a prettier way down, and a right of way to boot, between the houses clinging precariously to the cliff and this picture was taken using this particular route.

Nowadays Runswick Bay is the home of the second homers. Last time I asked there were precisely five houses which were occupied all year. I hope the purchasers took note of the happenings of 1682 when the whole village, with the exception of a single cottage, collapsed with the cliff into the sea.

Television viewers who remember watching the collapse of the Holbeck Hall Hotel just south of Scarborough suffer the same fate in 1993 will have some idea of the spectacle and a full realisation that this isn't an exaggeration.

In 1858 a small iron smelting works was destroyed and cracks started appearing in the houses in the village again in 1969. However a sea wall seems to have improved things and the import of the Norwegian stone which now protects the shoreline from the worst of the storms should extend the lifetime of the village.

The pub at the bottom – the Royal Hotel – has one of the finest prospects for a summer evening drink that I have seen in this country. Personally, I could sit here for hours and just watch the world go by on a summer's evening.

And indeed I have done just that, many times.

One of the pathways down to Runswick Bay

199

Fossils

This picture was taken at high tide. When the tide is out you can walk along the shale at the bottom of this outflow pipe. Without any effort on your part you will undoubtedly find fossils of the many strange creatures that lived here about 200 million years ago.

At that time this area was a large shallow sea and the erstwhile inhabitants were turned to impressions in the shale. Mostly they are ammonites of one sort or another resembling multi-compartmentalised snails, but there are also belemnites (a fossilised cuttlefish) and various bivalves – shellfish with a double shell such as the present day mussel or oyster.

More exotic fossils have also been found in this area including a dinosaur footprint, now in the museum at Whitby. Ancient marine reptiles, crocodiles, plesiosaurs with necks up to 40 feet long, ichthyosaurs and the long nosed crocodile-like stenosaurus and teleosaurus all thrived in these ancient seas. The land dinosaurs were also here or hereabouts leaving their footprints in the mud. When you walk along the rocks at Runswick you can be sure that a very long time ago what is now the shale under your feet was teeming with life of all shapes and sizes.

The sheer number of the fossils that have been found in one comparatively thin layer of shale is itself of interest and there has been speculation that some major polluting event caused the phenomenon.

Many of the ammonite type fossils are encased in what look like small boulders – concretions – and sometimes the outer rim just protrudes. The fossils along the beach are fair game but you shouldn't go digging into the cliffs for two reasons. Firstly sections of this coastline are designated sites of special scientific interest and technically you could find yourself in trouble. Secondly some of the cliffs are very unstable and are liable to deposit boulders of varying sizes on your head without provocation. To go hacking about into the unstable shales at the bottom of the cliffs can be dangerous and if it did come down on top of you then you would most definitely be in trouble of a different kind.

My kids crabbing at high tide in Runswick Bay

Gneiss Work

The coastal villages we pass through along this stretch of the walk have all suffered to a greater or lesser extent from the erosion of the cliffs.

Scarborough Borough Council has decided to act to prevent further erosion and the results can be seen to good effect here in Runswick. The rocks here replace the old sea defences which were made of concrete and crumbling. Take a look at the piers at Port Mulgrave and, to a lesser extent Skinningrove, to get a picture of what almost certainly lay in store for Runswick. The Borough's engineers estimated that the slipping cliffs were pushing the sea wall out to sea, in parts as much as an inch a week.

As a result, 464 concrete piles were sunk into the cliffs above the village to a depth of up to 25 metres and 19,000 boulders of ancient gneiss each weighing up to 12 tons were shipped from Norway and dumped on the beach at Runswick from a special barge.

These rocks have the effect of dissipating the waves as they come crashing in, absorbing the force the sea exerts on the wall. This ancient gneiss is probably the oldest rock you'll see on the Cleveland Way.

The engineering company AMEC who were contracted to carry out the work report that in the first few weeks their engineers were on site the sea wall was pushed out another six inches towards the sea. The car park was in danger of falling into the bay, and that would have, to all intents and purposes, put off the casual visitors to the village who, unlike us, aren't prepared to tackle the steep hill down from (and more to the point back up to) the cliff tops. The preservation work has also resulted in the construction of new car parks, one of which is for members of the Runswick Bay boat club, one for residents and a third for the rest of us.

Staithes has also benefited from this procedure as has Whitby, Robin Hood's Bay and Scarborough.

After you've had a scout round for fossils it's fun to spend a few idle minutes watching silly people stalling their cars while trying to climb the the 1-in-4 hill out of the village in too high a gear.

Runswick Bay and the stabilising boulders from Norway

Beach

Technically speaking the Cleveland Way now progresses along the beach at Runswick and up a little gully and back to the cliff tops. High tides can make this difficult unless you are a proficient under water walker, and in high seas this can be a risky operation. There isn't really an option to get around this and it's the only part of the Cleveland Way where the tides can be an issue. However, all is not lost. You can always while away the time, like Otis Redding, *"Sitting on the dock of the bay, watching the tide roll away"*.

On one of our many research visits to the Royal Hotel, we were eating in the upstairs dining room when just out of the window a herring gull was perched on top of a chimney. Nothing unusual about that. But this chimney had one of those revolving domes on it. The gull was spinning round like a ballerina, flicking its head from side to side, ballet fashion, to maintain focus. It fell off, and waddled off along the roof top like a drunk at closing time. As entertainment it would maybe not make a television series but Runswick Bay has furnished me with the only inkling I have as to what an inebriated seagull would look like.

The sands of Runswick Bay are always popular but never overloaded. The village itself is far too small to allow for much in the way of seaside commercialisation and indeed, other than the pub, the only retail establishment doubles as a small cafe and even then is not open all year.

Out of season, winter storms are dramatic and wild, although the replacement of the old sea wall with the energy absorbing rocks has ended the spectacle of high winds and high tides battering the concrete with the waves crashing over the top.

The picture opposite represents a typical August day on the beach with the clifftops providing a picturesque backdrop to the beach and the bay as it curves round to the headland at Kettleness Point. My kids call it the "Crocodile's Head". The view back to the village is every bit as pretty. It's not difficult to spend a lot of time here doing absolutely nothing in particular. For those of us who aren't at home on the crowded pleasure beaches of the big resorts, Runswick is a delightful contrast.

Birds

The Cleveland Way is a pleasant walk for bird spotters, its mixture of woodland, arable land, moorland and seaboard supplying a constant variety of opportunities to tick off species in a bird book.

These birds in the picture opposite are not gulls but fulmars. Fulmars breed in great numbers on the highest cliff-faces on the Yorkshire clifftops, usually with other cliff-nesting species. Outside the breeding season they are less attached to the mainland than many other seabirds. Very few members of the "tube-nosed" seabird family to which fulmars belong breed in the northern hemisphere – all their relatives breed south of the equator.

To defend their nest, fulmars launch an evil-smelling stream of projectile vomit consisting of stomach oils smelling like rotten fish. They lay a solitary egg, and it takes most of the summer to fledge the chick. Fulmars are very long lived – they can typically chalk up 50 years or more. They are foragers that travel up to hundreds of miles from the colony, eating surface species including squid, jellyfish, crustaceans, and small fish. They are expert in scavenging discarded fish thrown overboard by fishing boats – sometimes forming vast chattering groups of thousands of birds. They have thicker necks than gulls and fly with stiff straight, outstretched wings which makes them quite easy to spot as you walk along the cliffs and you are greeted by a bird rising slowly beside you on the updraught.

To the islanders of St Kilda the fulmar was an important economic resource. This island, far out in the Atlantic, 41 miles past the Outer Hebrides, was abandoned in 1936 because of the difficulty in communication and is now only inhabited by the military personnel working at the missile tracking station, who don't appear to have the same communication difficulties. The main seabird diet of these people (the native St Kildans, not the military) consisted of puffins and fulmars, and one estimate has it that the average St Kildan ate 115 fulmars per year. Whether this was as meat or for their oil is a moot point. They used to snack on puffins like we eat crisps. Catching these birds on the highest cliffs in Britain was quite an adventure.

Fulmars on the cliffs at Runswick Beach

Jet

The Cleveland Way follows the beach, past the boat houses, and up a steep pitched path in a gully back to the cliff top.

There are workings along here which are the residue of the old Jet industry.

Jet is a plant fossil – the result of the geological process on resinous ancient trees which resembled our modern day monkey puzzle. This tree was obviously widespread along much of the present line of the Cleveland Way – our first encounter with the old jet workings was way back near Carlton Bank.

Jet isn't found in large seams like ironstone – its occurrence is far more localised and unpredictable. It is found in "lenses" which are as small as a few inches and are never longer than a few feet. In situ it resembles coal, and may have been formed by similar processes, but jet is a different material. The differences between jet and coal may be due to the resin content of the original wood – about 10 gallons of oil can be extracted from a ton of jet shale. The old jet miners could spot likely places for the jet lenses by watching for the associated fossils. The ammonite Harpoceras – which is often found coated with iron pyrites – is found in the jet rocks. Jet can also be found loose on the beaches. To test whether you've got a piece of coal or jet, rub it along a rock. If the resulting mark is black it's coal. Jet leaves a brown trace.

Jet mining was carried out along this stretch of coastline mainly at Boulby, Staithes, Runswick and Sandsend. The miners were active between about 1840 and 1920 but jet jewellery fashion reached its height in Victorian times after the death of Prince Albert when Victoria went into an extended period of mourning. Her main choice for everything appears to have been black, which turned out to be a godsend for the locals hereabouts who cashed in with admirable entrepreneurism and made vast quantities of brooches, pendants and bangles. Fashion is transient, many would say fickle, and after a period of being out of sartorial favour, jet is once again in the ascendant.

There are still jet deposits in the cliffs but they are best left alone. These rocks are unstable.

The path back to Runswick from the cliff top towards Kettleness

Kettleness

Once more we have the remnants of the alum working industry below us as we make our way to the point at Kettleness.

This small settlement was home not just to alum workings and jet mining but also, to no-one's great surprise, ironstone production. Here it was extracted by quarrying from two seams, one 3ft thick and another at just over 2ft separated by a foot of shale. Ironstone was taken from the cliffs at beach level between 1838 and 1857. A further seam, to the east, was worked by drift between 1910 and 1915.

The site of the alum workings pictured opposite has been designated by English Heritage as a Scheduled Ancient Monument, but even the custodians of the nation's heritage are helpless against the ravages of the North Sea and deterioration of the site by erosion has led to a concerted attempt to record as much as possible about the workings before the sea gets to them.

Just along from Kettleness, near Goldsborough, there is a mound on the cliff top which is all that is left of a Roman signal station.

These were set up along the North East coast at the cliff high points. The Roman fleet had a big job on its hands supplying the garrisons along Hadrian's Wall. The main port for the wall is at Arbeia near South Shields where part of the fortifications have been reconstructed. Signals could be passed rapidly along the coastal stretch and, on the Cleveland Way, these stations were situated at Filey, Scarborough, Ravenscar, here at Goldsborough and Huntcliff near Saltburn. The Roman occupation reached Yorkshire in AD 71 and lasted until they were withdrawn by the Emperor Honorius in 410.

Time for a little piece of detective work. If you take a ruler to the OS map covering the eastern part of the Cleveland Way (OL27) and draw a line extending the "Roman Road" on Wheeldale in both directions the road links the Roman camp near Cropton with the East Cliff at Whitby. There doesn't seem to be any concrete evidence of records of a Roman station in Whitby but there is a very big gap between Ravenscar and Goldsborough, and you can't see one from the other. So maybe Whitby had one as well.

The "Roman Road" above is characterised in quotes because it is by no means certain that what we see is in fact Roman, but all the signs to it say "Roman Road" so in the absence of any agreed alternative, "Roman Road" will serve.

Vestiges of the Kettleness alum workings and the view back up the coast to Boulby

Tunnel

The Cleveland Way runs for a short distance alongside the track bed of the old railway. The track enters a tunnel here, re-emerges, passes through a second which ends just before Sandsend (the path descends by the tunnel at the other end) losing about 200ft in altitude above the sea level in the process.

Just inland from here is the village of Lythe which straddles the main coast road to Whitby. The Viking connection is in the name – *hlith* means slope in Old Scandinavian. The road down to Sandsend is a one-in-four with Mulgrave Castle on the right. Mulgrave Castle is the seat of the Lord of the Manor. It's an elegant castellated mansion, built in the middle of the 1700s. Within the grounds of the present day castle is the mediaeval Mulgrave Castle comprising a ruined keep, circular towers and a curtain wall dating from around 1200. It was extended in the 14th and 16th centuries but was partially dismantled in 1647 during the Civil War. This Mulgrave Castle was in turn the replacement for the even older Foss Castle.

The striking parish church, which is clearly visible from the cliff path, is dedicated to St Oswald. It was an ancient rectory but when Henry got his hands on it at the dissolution it passed into the Bygod (or Bigod)

family, then the occupants of Mulgrave Castle. Sir Francis Bygod had been made Ward to Cardinal Wolsey on the death of his grandfather. He appears to have been quite a machiavellian plotter and some say he was a spy. When Wolsey fell from grace Francis switched his allegiance to the unpleasant and ultimately doomed Thomas Cromwell. During the dissolution Francis plotted and schemed, interfering in the process of the dissolution of the great monastic institutions hereabouts for his own enrichment. He tried and failed to play both ends against the middle in the Pilgrimage of Grace. He was executed on June 2nd 1537. The church has been altered and rebuilt so many times that it isn't particularly easy to find out what it must have looked like in its early days. The tower dates from 1796 and the south side and porch were totally rebuilt in 1819. In all probability the origins of the church go back much further. It would appear that a wooden church was here before the Normans built one in stone. During a restoration in 1910 some Anglo-Danish stones were found and they are now exhibited in the church, proof, were it needed, that the religious presence on this site goes back a very long way.

More Alum

When we descend from the clifftops, partly courtesy of some wooden stairs that mitigate the worst effects of the descent, particularly in bad weather, the Cleveland Way follows the old railway trackbed around the headland and into Sandsend.

There are still more old alum workings here and the surroundings have that rather moonscape appearance. The car park that marks the transition from cliff path to metalled road is on the site of the old Alum House – the car park border stone work is all that remains of it.

Sandsend itself is a fairly pleasant spot with a few cafes and a beck which flows into the sea along the ravine. The Cleveland Way now becomes a choice of tarmac (the official path) or, at low tide, if you don't mind walking in sand, along the beach. This is only possible when the tides permit anyway – at high tides in high winds this stretch of road is pretty spectacular. Even walking on the pavement you can get very wet indeed.

The ground to the seaward side of the road is a golf course and hence out of bounds to the walker. The old railway line used to pass along where the golf course is now to West Cliff station, now no more. Sticking to the path, as we must less we incur the mighty wrath of the Whitby golfers, we bear left under the footbridge which is built so the golfers don't have too steep a climb, beneath the remains of the buttresses for the extinct railway line and then the path takes a rise up along the cliffs above the Whitby Upgang sands.

Technically the Cleveland Way takes the high ground here but again, provided the tides are favourable, the beach route provides an attractive option.

Eventually we reach the busy road which runs along the cliff tops with the Whitby hotels arranged in elegant rows and crescents on the right and brightly coloured wooden bathing huts far down on the beach below.

The Cleveland Way then passes by the statue of Captain Cook, under a whale bone arch – a memento of the days when Whitby was a major whaling port, down the Khyber Pass, to the quayside, bustling at all times of the year and on to the town centre of Whitby.

Sandsend Ness and Whitby in the distance

Whitby

There's quite a lot to say about Whitby and much of it is said elsewhere.

Streonshalh, as it was known to its Viking destroyers, has been a fishing port for many a long day and in the days before the ironclads it built ships. In 1828 it was the fifth biggest shipbuilding centre in England. Whitby colliers shipped coal from the North East fields to London and it was these sturdy, resilient ships with their flat bottoms and shallow draughts that James Cook chose for his voyages of exploration.

Cook came to Whitby from Staithes and his biographies are many and detailed and to repeat any of it here is a bit superfluous. Suffice to say that his first marine service was aboard the 1960s sounding *Freelove* and then to the *Three Brothers*, both Walker-owned ships. During unfavourable weather Cook studied astronomy, navigation and nautical law. His first command after he joined the Royal Navy was the *Sally* followed by spells with the *Solebay*, the *Pembroke* and the *Northumberland*. The *Sally* was re-named *Grenville* and this was the ship Cook used in his duties as marine surveyor for

Newfoundland. His first round the world trip was made in the *Endeavour* and thence the rest is history, and there's much of it in the Captain Cook Museum in Grape Lane, just across the swing bridge over the Esk on the right. This is supposed to be the house which James Cook lived in when he first came here.

The tall ship in the picture is berthed in the spot used by the modern day *Endeavour*, the Australian – built replica, which visited shortly after this picture was taken. The *Endeavour* will not be visiting Whitby again. Its last visit was in 2004 but the owners, the Government of Australia, wanted her back.

The Magpie cafe is on your right as you pass along the waterfront on the way to the swing bridge. This remarkable institution has queues of people outside at all times all year round awaiting the legendary fish and chips. Takes all kinds, I suppose. If queueing in the open isn't your idea of working up an appetite then there are many other fish and chip establishments in the town.

"Jean de la Lune" in Whitby harbour. More dramatic rain clouds

Easter

The earliest known mention of Whitby was by Bede, who tells us that a religious house was established here in or around 657AD by King Oswy of Northumbria. It was the place where the Synod of Whitby met in 664AD which decided to adopt the Roman form of Christianity rather than the Celtic form in Britain. St Hilda, formerly of Hartlepool, was the abbess during the Synod. The main difference we see nowadays is the way we calculate Easter Day. Our Easter is now the first Sunday after the first full moon after the vernal equinox. Many other traditions and rituals were also consigned to Celtic history, but most of these concerned the religious communities rather than the populace at large.

In 867 the Abbey was destroyed by the Danes together with most of the rest of the settlement. They rebuilt it and it became the centre of a small Danish colony. William the Conqueror trashed it as part of his Harrying, and then Henry I made a grant to the abbot and convent of Whitby of a burgage in the village, probably as part of some kind of reparation for wrongs inflicted. Henry I also granted the abbot of Whitby a fair on the feast of St Hilda. Richard de Waterville, who was abbot between 1175 and 1190, granted the town in free burgage to the burgesses. This more or less meant that the haves of the town formally had the town. This was confirmed in 1200 by King John, who had been bribed by the burgesses, but in 1201, after another bribe, this time from the successor of Richard de Waterville, he quashed it as injurious to the dignity of the church of Whitby. Nothing to do with the bribes, then. A struggle went on until the 14th century when a trial resulted in a judgment against the burgesses. The church didn't get its own way for long. Two hundred years later it lost all its monasteries.

Between the years 1674 – 1675 the Crown, thankful for the part played by the Cholmleys in the Civil War, restored to the lords of the manor all the liberties enjoyed by the abbots of Whitby. A market was held on Sundays until the reign of Henry VI, who changed the day to Saturday which is as it stands today. A fortnightly cattle market was granted by Charles I.

There was a port at Whitby in the 12th century and probably before then. The salting of herrings started in mediaeval times and kipper production is carried out today most famously by Fortunes whose smokery is past the 199 steps in Henrietta Street, a short but interesting detour from the Cleveland Way.

Whitby in the sunshine after a rain squall from the top of the 199 steps

Vampire

Resisting the temptation to blow our walking funds in the amusement arcades we pass over the swing bridge then through the old town to the 199 steps up to the abbey. Count them if you like – it's right. At the top of the steps is the abbey and the church with this graveyard (pictured opposite).

Bram Stoker, a Dubliner, was on a brief holiday in Whitby in the summer of 1890 when he visited the library and borrowed a book catchingly entitled *"An Account of the Principalities of Wallachia and Moldavia (1820)"* by William Wilkinson. Stoker took notes – now part of his papers housed at the Rosenbach Museum in Philadelphia – including a section on one "Voivode (Count) Dracula" who fought against the Turks. A footnote noted that "Dracula in the Wallachian language means Devil" and so we got Christopher Lee hamming it up as Dracula rather than "Wampyr", the original name for the bloodsucker.

A Russian schooner named *Demetrius* had foundered off Whitby's coast in 1885, tipping its cargo of occupied coffins into the sea. This charming incident, no doubt as related to Stoker by the burgesses of Whitby, was quite obviously an influence because Dracula arrives in Whitby on the *Demeter* with all on board dead and the captain lashed to the wheel. Spooky.

Dracula then escapes in the form of a huge black dog. According to vampire experts vampires cannot cross running water except at the turn of the tide. Apparently. He hides in a grave (where else?) in St. Mary's churchyard where he later attacks Lucy, his first conquest in an illustrious book and film career, if only he knew it at the time.

There is a "Dracula Experience" on the quay front which apparently scares little ones. You may arrive in Whitby at a time when the town is garlanded with Dracula lookalikes posing around the town in all their gothic finery. I'd like to be able to say that they all know it's only a story, but sometimes I can't convince myself that it's actually the case.

Still, as long as they only bite each other and leave the rest of us alone, who cares? Makes a change from fish and chips, I suppose.

Graveyard on the cliff at Whitby. Dracula was here

221

Abbey and House

Here we are again – Henry VIII revisited for the umpteenth and last time along the Cleveland Way. Henry's handiwork is here for all to see for miles around in the form of the ruined abbey. He wasn't the first one to reduce Whitby Abbey to rubble – an earlier building had been razed by the Vikings in 870 – but at least they had the excuse that there was neither sham nor pretence, just a good old fashioned Viking party of rape and pillage, fire and sword.

The abbey was founded by Oswy, King of Northumbria, in 657 (according to English Heritage – other dates are given elsewhere) to fulfil a vow for a victory over Penda, King of Mercia. It was an establishment for monks and (until the Conquest) for nuns of the Benedictine Order. Under Hilda, a grand-niece of Edwin, a former king of Northumbria, it became such a prominent establishment of the Celtic church that it was chosen by Oswy to host the synod of 664, ushering in the Roman Catholicism of St Augustine.

The existing ruins date largely from the thirteenth century and consist of the remnants of the Early English choir, the north transept which is also Early English but of a later date, and the Decorated nave.

The west side of the nave fell down in 1763 and the tower followed in 1830. The foundations of cloisters and domestic buildings are to the south.

The Cholmleys acquired the abbey in 1539. The imposing hall next to the abbey was built in about 1580 from the materials lifted from the monastic buildings. It was enlarged and fortified by Sir Hugh Cholmley around 1635 with the proceeds from his involvement with the alum industry and the building of a fortified harbour in Tangiers.

In 1997 a rare and, remarkably, almost intact formal garden decorated with cobbles, pebbles and stones from the beach was unearthed at the front of the house which has now been uncovered and opened to the public. The Cholmleys paid £232,000 for their mansion – an absolute fortune for the time. It was finished in 1672.

223

Poet's Corner

In the churchyard is the memorial to the poet Caedmon who started life as a cowherd to St Hilda at the abbey. The Venerable Bede takes up the story of the first "English" poet whose works have been preserved, reproduced here in translation to Modern English....

'In the monastery at Whitby lived a brother singularly gifted by God's grace. So skilful was he in composing religious and devotional songs that, when any passage of the Bible was explained to him by interpreters, he could quickly turn it into delightful and moving poetry in his own English tongue. These verses of his have stirred the hearts of many to despise the world and aspire to heavenly things. Others after him have tried to compose religious poems in English, but none could compare with him; for he did not acquire the art of poetry from men or through any human teacher, but received it as a free gift from God. For this reason he could never compose any frivolous or profane verses; only such as had a religious theme fell from his lips.

He had followed a secular occupation until well advanced in years, without learning anything about poetry. Indeed it sometimes happened at a feast that all the guests in turn would be invited to sing and entertain the company; then, when he saw the harp coming his way, he would get up from the table and go home.

On one such occasion he left the house in which the entertainment was being held and went out to the stable, where it was his duty that night to look after the beasts. There, when the time came, he settled down to sleep. Suddenly in a dream he saw a man standing beside him who called him by name.

"Caedmon," he said, "sing me a song."

"I don't know how to sing," he replied, "It is because I cannot sing that I left the feast and came here."

The man who addressed him then said: "But you shall sing to me."

"What should I sing about?"

"Sing about the Creation of all things," the other answered.

And Caedmon immediately began to sing verses in praise of God the Creator that he had never heard before.'

225

Wreck

The *Rohilla* was a 7,400 ton ship that began life on the London to Calcutta service. She had had her 15 minutes of fame – along with her sister ship the *Rewa* she had represented British India at King George V's review of the fleet at Spithead in 1910. *Rewa* carried the House of Commons, *Rohilla* the Lords. On the 6th of August 1914 the *Rohilla* was requisitioned by the government and converted for use as a Hospital Ship. On the 29th of October she left Leith bound for Dunkirk to pick up wounded soldiers but at 0400 the next day she ran aground here by Saltwick Nab, lost her way, ran onto the bank and the ensuing storm broke her back.

Six lifeboats from stations as far apart as Tynemouth and Scarborough were involved over a period of two and a half days trying to rescue the 229 crew and medical staff on board.

It was impossible to launch the Whitby No1 Lifeboat and row her to the wreck so the No2 – the *John Fielden*, which was kept afloat in the harbour, was dragged across the sands and launched at 7am. It reached the *Rohilla* with great difficulty and a total of 35 people were rescued in two trips but the boat was so badly damaged it couldn't be used again. The Upgang lifeboat was lowered down the cliffs but the sea was so bad it couldn't reach *Rohilla*. Scarborough's lifeboat *Queensbury* was towed to Saltwick by a steam trawler. By this time darkness had fallen. The boat waited 18 hours overnight but couldn't reach the *Rohilla*. It returned to Scarborough. The Teesside lifeboat *Bradford IV* tried to get there but it was damaged. Its crew had to be rescued by a tug. On the morning of the 31st the *Robert & Mary Ellis* lifeboat, launched from Whitby, awaited a tow from *Mayfly*, a steam trawler from Hartlepool. They couldn't get within half a mile. At 9 o'clock *William Riley*, the Upgang lifeboat, made an unsuccessful rescue attempt. At 4:15pm the *Henry Vernon*, a motor lifeboat, left Tynemouth, arriving at 1am on 1st November. At 6:30am they discharged oil on the sea, and managed to recover 40 men. Both it and *Rohilla* were hit by two huge waves. It managed to get another 10 men off before withdrawing.

Nabbed

The following RNLI Medals were awarded in respect of the *Rohilla* rescue:

Gold medals to Cox Thomas Langlands of Whitby, Cox Robert Smith of Tynemouth and Captain Burton of Tynemouth

Silver medals to 2nd Cox Richard Eglon of Whitby, 2nd Cox James Brownlee of Tynemouth, Lieutenant Basil Hall and George Peart, who had repeatedly helped men who had managed to swim ashore from the wreck

"RNLI Thanks on Vellum" were awarded to Cox Pounder Robinson of Upgang and 2nd Cox T.Kelly of Upgang.

Monetary awards were made to all the Lifeboatmen involved and to the crews of the two trawlers which had acted as tugs.

Major Burton of the Tynemouth lifeboat was awarded an Empire Gallantry Medal on the 30th of June 1924 for his bravery, this was later changed to a George Cross in 1940 when the award was instituted.

84 members of the ship's compliment lost their lives out of a total of 229.

The *Rohilla* – what's left of it as it is today – sits in an east – west orientation below the sea with the inshore end usually in about 6 metres and the seaward end in around 15 metres of water. It isn't visible from the cliffs.

The nab on the picture has the familiar look of alum workings, which isn't surprising because that's exactly what they are.

The Italians had one big secret regarding the production of alum and that was how to judge the right time to drain off the supernatant liquor to give a maximum yield of the final product. If you weren't paying attention back at Boulby you'll have to read it again.

The big secret was smuggled out of Italy and to England enabling alum makers in these fair islands to thumb their noses at the pope without fear of worldly redress. The secret? See if a fresh egg floats in it.

The Concrete and the Clay

As we follow the path along the cliffs the other side of the camping and caravan site we are suddenly overlooking a strange wreck, visible at low tide.

This is all that remains of the *Creteblock*.

This strange vessel was a "concrete lighter". It was commissioned towards the end of the first World War when a shortage of steel provided the impetus for this unlikely marine construction material.

It wasn't, however, a new idea.

The World Exhibition of 1854 in Paris had witnessed the first ever concrete boat. It was a rowing boat, the brainchild of a M. Lambot, and quite obviously not a roaring success because it was the beginning and end of a production run of one.

Undaunted by the apparent unsuitability of the material for building ocean going vessels, a Dutchman, Zementeisen-Fabrik Gebruder Picha-Stevens, built a sloop in 1887 which was marginally bigger than M. Lambot's rowing boat, and an American, one Daniel D. Banks, built a schooner in 1892. The Italians (1905), the Germans (1908), the British and Dutch (1910) and the Norwegians (1913) all started building concrete boats and the fashion spread – by 1911 there were several of them plying their trade on the Panama Canal.

The Admiralty eventually took the material seriously and by 1917 there were programmes for building tugs and barges of concrete, one of the uses of the barges being to ferry iron ore from Spain.

The Navy's total orders for these craft eventually numbered 154 but only 17 of them were built, and the *Creteblock*, a tug, was one of them.

She was bought by Smith's Dock in Middlesbrough and worked on the Tees until 1935 when she was moved to Whitby.

For a time she was used as a fishermen's store but her time was coming to an end.

Increasingly, as more and more bits fell off, she became an eyesore and the company was instructed to get rid of her. She was patched up to make her seaworthy in order that she could be towed out to sea and scuttled. This idea was completely successful until the point when it actually had to be put into practice. She started taking in water immediately and was beached just around the corner, by Saltwick Nab, not far from where the *Rohilla* lies.

A load of old bull

The white building on the cliff edge with its two huge horns on the top is an old fog warning system that used to bellow out a low frequency booming noise to warn shipping of the dangerous rocks and cliffs. It was known variously as the Whitby Fog Warning Station (on the OS maps), the Whitestone Point Fog Warning Station or by its nickname of the "Hawsker Bull". The fog hasn't gone as you may well be unfortunate enough to experience, but modern navigation systems and radio beacons have rendered the old bull as redundant as artificial insemination did for the real, four legged variety.

Hawsker comes in two flavours, High Hawsker and, something of a surprise, Low Hawsker. The OS map even adds plain old Hawsker making a threesome.

The views and the walking around this part of the walk are as good as it gets along the coastal section, particularly on a fine clear day.

Hawsker is credited as the place where George Fox "founded" the Society of Friends, often known by the slightly derogatory "Quakers". Fox was an itinerant preacher and certainly spent some time around these parts. His philosophy, incorporating such dangerous ideas as pacifism, equality of men and women, the denial of the necessity for an ordained clergy and the refusal to doff the cap to his betters – among other things – naturally made him enemies in the highest places and laid his followers open to persecution from both the Puritan Cromwellians and the Episcopalians of the restored monarchy under Charles II. 1654 is given as the Hawsker date but the Friends themselves appear to hold a 1652 incident at Swathmoor Hall, home of Judge Thomas Fell, near Morecambe as a defining moment in their evolution into a formal organisation. Neither the judge, who was out on the circuit, nor his wife were at home and Fox spent some time talking with the local priest, one William Lampitt. Lampitt didn't want Fox at the hall, hardly surprising, really, as Fox referred to him as "a man full of filth", presumably within Lampitt's hearing. On the face of it Fox could maybe have taught the old master John Knox a thing or two when it came to righteous invective.

The "Hawsker Bull" – once a foghorn and the cliff path once again close to the edge

Another rescue

Another famous lifeboat rescue took place along this coast on 19 January 1881, in a way even more remarkable than that of the *Rohilla*.

At 10.30 am on 19 January 1881 Captain Robert Gibson who was Harbour Master at Whitby received a telegram reporting that a ship – the Whitby Brig *Visitor* – had sunk off Robin Hood's Bay. Her crew had taken to the ship's lifeboat but had been forced to drop anchor. There had been several days of heavy snowfall and they were unable to reach land because of very heavy seas. The ferocity of the wind and the heaving sea at Whitby made it impossible for the Whitby Lifeboat to be launched and rowed around the rocky coast to Robin Hood's Bay. The lifeboatmen decided to drag the lifeboat the 6 miles overland to Robin Hood's Bay and launch it from there. This was no mean undertaking – dragging a heavy lifeboat over very narrow roads and across moorland some 500 feet above sea level in drifting snow up to 7 feet deep.

About sixty Whitby men took shovels and began digging to clear the snow from the roads. Horses were brought out and hitched to the lifeboat carriage and the *Robert Whitworth* set off on her journey overland to Robin Hood's Bay. Overall some 200 men helped at one stage or another in the work to clear the snow. More horses – eighteen eventually – were commandeered from farmers along the way. Men from Robin Hood's Bay started digging from their end working to clear the snow and after 2 hours hard slog the lifeboat was lowered down the steep hill into the village.

The crew of the lifeboat had been working along the way clearing the snow with the rest. They then manned the boat and set out on the rescue at sea. Before they got there 6 of the boat's oars and the steering oar were smashed by a heavy wave and they had to return to shore. While the oars were being replaced the Cox, Henry Freeman, asked for volunteers to double bank the oars and the lifeboat set out, this time with 18 men. After an hour and a half they managed to reach the sailors in the small boat, and landed them at Robin Hood's Bay at 4pm. Maybe not the sheer scale of the *Rohilla*, but another remarkable tale of real heroism.

The path approaching Robin Hood's Bay

We meet again

It's around this point that we're joined again by the Coast-to-Coast walk for its final few miles to its end in Robin Hood's Bay.

While we've stuck to the high escarpments of the North York Moors and North Sea cliffs, the Coast to Coast followed the old ironstone railway with the Lyke Wake Walk and then left it at the head of Rosedale, over the moors, down Fryupdale, into the Esk Valley then out again over the moors finally arriving at the last section of the walk on the high cliffs near Hawsker.

The two paths, now congruent, continue along the cliff edge towards Baytown. Occasionally the track takes us down, as in the picture opposite, almost to sea level, across small becks and back up the other side, over stiles and through fences. For a brief 200 yards or so the Cleveland Way departs from the cliff edge, bypassing the promontory at Normanby Stye Batts before once again returning to its perch along the cliff edge looking down to the sea and the multitude of seabirds.

Finally rounding the headland at Ness Point, Robin Hood's Bay hoves into view and the vista stretches out over the bay to Ravenscar.

The cliffs from Whitby to Robin Hood's Bay provide a good straightforward stretch of walking and a steady end to the journey for the Coast to Coasters as they see the finish of their trek finally open out below them.

We leave the cliff path behind us and take once more to the tarmac to start the descent into Robin Hood's Bay and a natural break point in the Way.

However, there is one thing to do before we get to Robin Hood's Bay. Whitby was the home for almost seventy years to a man from Leeds who has left us a unique legacy of superb images of the middle Victorian age to just before the outbreak of World War II. Now's the time for a quick look at a man who recorded this stretch of coastline, the villages, the ships and the people, mainly between Staithes and Robin Hood's Bay, starting in 1870 more or less until his death. A remarkable Victorian photographer by the name of Frank Meadow Sutcliffe, FRPS.

Meadow

Henry Fox Talbot made the earliest known surviving photographic negative on paper in the late summer of 1835, a small photograph of a window in his home. His reported work was read to a meeting of the Royal Society on 31 January 1839. The paper was entitled 'An Account of the Art of Photogenic Drawing or the process by which natural objects may be made to delineate themselves without the aid of the artist's pencil.' And so photography as we know it today was born.

Frank Meadow Sutcliffe was born in Headingley, Leeds in 1853, the son of Thomas Sutcliffe, an artist, lecturer and art critic. Sutcliffe senior was probably one of the first camera owners in Leeds, and his son was encouraged to explore this new medium. With his father's analytical artist's expertise helping him along he used the camera as a creative tool rather than simply a recording device.

The Sutcliffes moved to Whitby in 1870 and Thomas died the following year. Frank, by now the family breadwinner, returned to Whitby after an unsuccessful attempt at setting up a photographic studio in Tunbridge Wells. His Whitby studio was set up in a disused jet workshop where he managed to succeed in making a living in his new medium but he had a habit of taking the morning off to go out and capture local people and scenes.

It is these photographs that are sold worldwide as prints and books from the Sutcliffe Gallery in Whitby. The technical quality of the pictures is outstanding for the time. They were taken using a plate camera made of mahogany and brass, mounted on a heavy wooden tripod, and the pictures were recorded on glass plates. Typically on his jaunts he would carry around 6 plates each mounted in wooden slides.

Because of the limitations of the Victorian emulsions all of his portraits, though they don't immediately look it, were carefully posed with the subjects holding absolutely still in their positions for many seconds. Take a look at the lifeboatmen and fishermen – these were the contemporaries of the heroes of the *Rohilla* and the *Visitor*. Frank Meadow Sutcliffe died aged 88 in 1941.

Robin Hood

Precisely what the mediaeval outlaw legend had to do with this picturesque village, crammed in at the bottom of a wyke under the high cliffs of North Yorkshire isn't clear.

In fact no record exists of a settlement here until the sixteenth century, with a big expansion in 1538. This was around 340 years after the Merry Men in their Lincoln Green were thumbing their noses at the Sheriff of Nottingham and plighting their troth to the Good King Richard in his battles with his little brother the Bad Prince John. It was formerly known, and is still by the locals today, as Baytown. There are Bronze Age burial mounds about a mile to the south of the village which are known as Robin Hood's Butts. A remarkable prescience as they pre-dated Friar Tuck by some two thousand years.

As in most of these coastal villages the main industry until the early years of the 20th century was fishing, and now is tourism. Around 1820 there were 130 fishermen sailing 35 cobles and 5 big herring boats but by 1920 there were just two fishing families left.

Baytown is no different to Staithes, Runswick or Kettleness in its vulnerability to the eroding North Sea. In 1780 a severe storm caused 22 of the houses in King

Street to collapse into the sea and a decade or so later some of Park Road went the same way. Now Robin Hood's Bay boasts the highest sea wall in Britain – 40 feet high and 500 feet long, as can be seen on careful scrutiny of the picture opposite.

The steep walk down into the village – off limits to motorists – is a pleasant change from the clifftop path, and anyway it won't be long before we're back up there with the fulmars and gulls.

The village, like many on the coast, was heavily involved in smuggling which was more or less institutionalised, only dying out with the relaxation of excise duties. Legends abound of secret tunnels and one says that it is possible to travel from the shore to the top of the hill without once surfacing.

The Coast-to-Coast walk ends here with the traditional dipping of booted feet into the sea.

Anyone wanting more information about this village could do worse than investing in "A History of Robin Hood's Bay" by Barrie Farnill (ISBN 1 904622 04 6) which gives a detailed account of the settlement from the earliest times. It is illustrated with photographs from the Robin Lidster Collection.

Robin Hood's Bay and Ravenscar in the haze

241

Fossiling

Of all the Jurassic fossil records in the area this one is probably the most fertile and extensive.

The rocks on the shore below were laid down over a ten million year period about 180 million years ago, well into the dinosaur period of Jurassic Park but 100 million years or so before Tyrannosaurus Rex.

At low tide, there is about 1800 feet of sea floor exposed which makes for interesting fossil hunting and tide pool investigation. The Cleveland Way wisely takes to the cliffs but there is nothing stopping you walking to Ravenscar at low tide when the three miles of beach is exposed. However, the tide turns quickly and you can get cut off in very short order. It's a fair old scramble up the cliffs – if indeed you make it. We've seen how brave the lifeboat folk are hereabouts but I doubt you'd get much in the way of thanks for providing the visiting tourists with a live demonstration of their skills. During high spring tides the sea can force its way up the main village street, which actually asks for trouble by ending in the sea by The Bay Hotel (the Coast-to-Coast's final watering hole).

This area between Robin Hood's Bay and Ravenscar is of national, and indeed international importance for the fossil records contained and for its accessiblity for exploration. The field trip here is one of many that are undertaken by schools, universities and amateur geological societies investigating this fascinating era of plant and marine fossil evolution.

More than 250 species of fossils from over 600 beds have been identified from this area. There are organised fossil hunts with children in mind taking place here and at Sandsend, Runswick Bay, Ravenscar and Scalby. It isn't a bad idea, particularly with youngsters, to stick to one of these organised groups. Not only will you get expert help in finding, identifying and caring for the fossils, the trips are timed to work with the tide timetables and they will also steer you clear of the dangerous parts of the cliffs which are generally unstable – rock falls are not uncommon.

Back to the Way.

243

Boggling

Boggle Hole is one of the many dips in the coastal path where the Cleveland Way descends to the shoreline. Boggle Hole is unique in that it's the only one with a Youth Hostel there waiting for you. The hostel used to be a corn mill and has "flexible opening" for most of the year outside the high summer and Christmas periods. If you are intending to make use of the facilities you're advised to get in touch 48 hours before your intended arrival. Many of its rooms are in a newer annexe.

Boggle Hole is one of several parts of the Heritage Coast owned and cared for by the National Trust. The major Trust holdings along the path include the very start of the coastal section at Old Saltburn, Warsett Hill where the Boulby Mine Mineral railway line skirts the clifftops, the cliffs above Hummersea and Boulby, Cowbar Nab at Staithes, Port Mulgrave, part of the cliff on the way into Runswick Bay, Saltwick Nab near Whitby, the cliffs as you turn the headland on the route to Robin Hood's Bay – all places so far visited – and to come Ravenscar, Hayburn Wyke and the northern cliffs at Cayton Bay.

Most of the historic buildings near to the Cleveland Way are in the care of English Heritage. The only National Trust historic buildings which charge entry within a mile or two of the path are Mount Grace Priory. and the Rievaulx Terraces up from Helmsley. It's worth noting that although Mount Grace Priory is owned by the National Trust it is managed by English Heritage so members of both organisations benefit from free entry. Other than that the nearest National Trust offering is Ormesby Hall on the south end of Middlesbrough, just over six miles from Roseberry Topping, the nearest point to Ormesby on the Cleveland Way. Roseberry Topping is itself also owned by the National Trust.

A Boggle is a name for a hobgoblin, but the main inhabitants of this little hideaway were in reality more likely cut throat smugglers. A better den you'd be pushed to find.

Looking back to Robin Hood's Bay from Boggle Hole

Bay

The Cleveland Way left Robin Hood's Bay along a climb between the tumbling houses to a path above the beach and out onto the cliffs. Between here and Ravenscar the cliffs are lower than before and are steeply sloping rather than sheer, so the walking is easy. After Boggle Hole the path climbs once again but it's not far before another dip into Stoupe Beck and then up again to the cliffs.

Stoupe Beck is an unlikely site for oil exploration, but in 1997 Morrison Middlefield Resources Limited went drilling for oil around here under the terms of its North Yorkshire Licence. Judging by the lack of oil rigs it would appear they were less than successful.

The alum industry was also at work near here. An old quarry on Stoupe Brow about half a mile due south of here was the site of alum shale excavation and we'll pass the site of the works on the way into Ravenscar. The quarrying started in about 1650 and continued working until about 1850. The scale of alum production along this coast can be gauged by the fact that in all probability, in the peak year of production around 1768,

over one hundred thousand tons of rock a year were dug out by pickaxe and shovel and moved in wheelbarrows along the alum manufacturing line. Over the course of the whole production lifetime there must have been millions of tons of Heritage Coast cliffs shifted in what must have seemed at times like a 40 mile long thin anthill. There are two quarries, the nearest one to Ravenscar is National Trust owned.

These old quarries can be seen to best effect if you fancy the circular walk along the cliffs between Robin Hood's Bay and Ravenscar and back along the disused railway line. You can still see the old track beds and there is an information board helpfully provided by the National Trust about the history of the old alum industry.

An excavation as long ago as 1771 revealed that one of the mounds is an ancient burial site. More recent excavations have discovered Bronze Age urns. They are are in the care of Scarborough Museums and Gallery.

Peak

Unlike most of the place names along the Cleveland Way, Ravenscar is a newcomer. Prior to 1897 it was known simply as "Peak". Welcome to the "Town that Never Was".

Your first inkling and a clue to what went on here at the end of the nineteenth and the beginning of the twentieth century will come by watching the path itself. Embedded in it hereabouts are bricks with "RAVENSCAR" indented in them. The Whitaker Brick Company started making Ravenscar bricks in 1900 which were to be used in the construction of a proposed new seaside holiday development. The works were situated on the site of the alum quarry and were conveniently at hand for sidings connecting the railway line that had arrived here in 1885.

A company by the name of the "Ravenscar Estate Company" bought the Peak estate in 1895 for the sum of £10,000 in order to build a seaside resort. Now, I know that sometimes I'm slow on the uptake, but it would take some leap of the imagination to think that people would come on a beach holiday to a village 630 feet above sea level atop inaccessible cliffs. Look down when you get there. There isn't a beach under Ravenscar. Undaunted, streets were laid out, services installed and plots sold at auction. The Raven Hall Hotel has some of the auction details framed on the walls of its public rooms. Special trains were laid on by the company to bring speculative investors from the industrial heartlands to see for themselves the potential of the development.

Unfortunately for the Ravenscar Estate Company they did just that. What just about everybody other than – it would seem – the Company owners saw as rather obvious was also the view of the potential buyers and investors. The plots went unsold and as night follows the day, the Ravenscar Estate Company folded in 1913.

Although the resort never materialised, the brickworks made the best of the poor hand it had been dealt and went on making bricks for a while, supplying the material for the 'Northstead' housing estate and the Odeon Cinema in Scarborough during the 1930s.

Railway

Just before you get to Ravenscar you pass alongside the hotel's golf course. It's possibly the most unlikely location for a golf course that you'll see in this country, although I'm sure that someone will know better. Whoever thought of putting a golf course on these cliffs certainly deserves a gold star for lateral thinking.

On the right hand side of the path as it enters Ravenscar is the rail track which wends its way back to Robin Hood's Bay making a reasonable circular walk. The railway was opened in 1885 and one of the main benefactors was the owner of the Raven Hall Hotel, one Mr. William Hammond, a Londoner. Mr Hammond had bought the hall in 1845 and became an enthusiastic supporter and director of the railway building project. His enthusiasm for the line didn't extend to having it in his back yard though. As it passed his 300 acre holding he insisted that it went under a tunnel, which was duly built at an additional cost of £500. Ravenscar had its own railway station until 1965. It was built as part of the abandoned Ravenscar development.

Most of the length of the old trackbed of the Whitby to Scarborough railway is not a right of way but is a permissive bridleway, owned by Scarborough Borough Council with permission for walkers, cyclists and riders to use it as a recreational path.

Should you get the bus either to start or to end the Ravenscar section you may end up in the bus turning circle, which is a short walk on the metalled road running inland. parallel to the Cleveland Way. This area is next to the platform of the now defunct Ravenscar railway station. At the entrance to the platform Vivien Moudsell has executed two sculptures depicting platform people from days gone by. On the left, looking towards the platform, we see a parent with a child awaiting a train – or perhaps waving off a loved one – and the other sculpture on the right shows an arm raised, whistle-to-mouth guard signalling imminent departure accompanied by the station dog. As part of the project she worked with local youngsters making tiles depicting the old railway in its heyday.

Vivien Moudsell has done other work along this coast, again slightly off the Cleveland Way, at Kettleness, where a sculpted seat sits on a lovely viewpoint over Runswick Bay. This was done as part of the North York Moors National Park's Community Rail Paths Project to commemorate the Millennium. She also executed the start and end markers for the Cleveland Way as well as the stone Heritage Coast marker on the path out of Saltburn.

Display of pink and white foxgloves by the abandoned Scarborough to Whitby railway

Radar

The Hotel is used to hikers and welcomes walkers for a drink and a bite to eat, should you wish to avail yourself of its services. Not far from here, at the radio mast just outside Ravenscar, is the end of road for the souls who've managed to brave the the body-sapping Lyke Wake Walk. You may be privileged to witness these joyous folk as they happily skip along for some light refreshment after their 42-miles-in-less-than-24-hour bash over the high moors. One of these days I might try it, but every time I start to contemplate it I ask a simple question. Why? The challenge, I suppose, the sense of achievement. The limbs that won't work. The cold, the dark and the loneliness of the high moors. The organisation, the support groups, the pathway knee deep in mud....

Back along these here cliffs, and occasionally elsewhere on this section of the Cleveland Way, you'll find relics of the world wars in the shape of coastal defences. On this section there is a pill box, slipping slowly into the sea, and back near Boulby there is an old sound mirror which was built in 1916 to warn of Zeppelin raids.

The Boulby concrete structure was the forerunner of radar in function if not in technology. It was a large (about 15 ft diameter) parabolic concrete dish which was used to amplify sound waves. It is on land belonging to one of the farms on the clifftop and can't be seen directly from the Cleveland Way path although its back is visible from the clifftop road.

The Romans built a fort on the cliffs here at Ravenscar but there's nothing left other than a stone in Whitby museum. It was built over by the hotel and it's not beyond the realms of possibility that some of the old Roman stones are incorporated into the fabric of the building. A translation of the inscription on the stone is

"Justinian, governor of the province, and Vindician, general of the forces of Upper Britain, for the second time, with the younger provincial soldiers built this fort, the manager of public works giving his assistance."

Just after the Conquest the land here was granted to the Knights Hospitaller and after the dissolution some of their privileges passed on to the new freeholders.

View of Robin Hood's Bay and Baytown from the battlements of the Raven Hall Hotel

Madness

This rather splendid hotel in a quite unique setting was built in 1774 by Captain William Childs of the King's Regiment of Light Dragoons who came from London to Yorkshire during his army service. He had come into ownership of the alum works in 1763 and presumably liked the spot and decided to settle here with his family.

He died in 1829 and the building passed to his daughter, Ann Willis. Her husband Francis, an Oxford graduate, had made a small fortune in treating George III with many of the standard methods of the period including coercion, restraint in a strait jacket and blistering. Willis was said to have more kindness and consideration for the patient than was usual and the King's recovery in 1789 made Willis' reputation. It has to be said that despite the many claims that George himself was secretly treated here it is very unlikely to be true.

Their son Richard Willis soon saw to the family fortune. A man of the cloth, the Rev. Dr Willis was a gambling addict with particular passions for horse racing and louse racing. Yes – lice. His spendthrift ways soon saw off his inheritance and he devised a crafty income scheme to charge a guinea a time for a hypnotic cure for insomnia. He was a man ahead of his time. Nowadays he would be hailed by some of the wilder alternative medical practitioners as an icon.

His main contribution to the hotel's surroundings was the construction of the hanging gardens. This was accomplished quite straightforwardly by blasting them out of the cliff.

This eccentric gambler was eventually turfed out of the hall by William Hammond (see the bit about the railway) who foreclosed on a mortgage in 1845. It has been said that he lost the hotel betting on a woodlouse race with a saucer as the course. It may well be the way he lost his money but Mr Hammond came into the hall by altogether more conventional means.

After his death in 1890 his daughters sold it to the development company and it was opened as an hotel in 1895. The hotel has been used by the armed forces as a wartime billet and a past owner moored a steamship in the bay.

Cliffs

It is wise not to get too refreshed at the hotel. The reasons will shortly become apparent as you set off out on the path towards Scarborough.

The trail sets off up the road towards the ghostly remnants of the grand development. All that came to pass were these few houses and a railway station.

We are heading back to the clifftops along the deserted never-was town roads. Once we regain the cliff path our track is initially a path between a high hedgerow and a farm's fields. Soon we're back on the cliffs with the exhilarating views back, forward and out to sea. Occasionally the path is flanked on both sides with vegetation which is too high to see over. After climbing one of the steeper parts with this high undergrowth on both sides all of a sudden you are at the top, out in the open with no shrubbery or any other impediments to the seaward. At this point we're not as high as we were at Boulby – the cliffs here are about 450 feet high – but the views are sensational and I can say that it quite literally took my breath away.

We are now at the highest point on the path south of Ravenscar and the Cleveland Way begins its gradual downward progress to the big seaside resort.

The cliffs around Ravenscar have yielded many Dinosaur Footprints. The first was recorded by the Ravenscar Group as long ago as 1906 but it was a while before serious geologists regarded them as little more than curiosities. More recently it has been shown that the footprints are more common and more varied in type than had previously been supposed. The Jurassic footprints present in these rocks not only tell us about the size and gait of these creatures but also provide important information about the climate and the environment in which they lived. In the middle Jurassic a great diversification was taking place. Worldwide there is little in the way of skeletal remains and these sites along the Yorkshire coast have contributed important information.

It's not long before the headland at Scarborough comes into view from the Ravenscar summit – unmistakable with the castle ruins atop the promontory which separates Scarborough's busy, loud and bustling South Bay from the rather more relaxed North Bay.

Looking down from the Ravenscar cliff top

Ambulance

As we can see from the picture opposite the path continues between the fences and the cliff edge. Navigation isn't a problem.

Much of the land to the west of here was held from the time of Henry I to the Dissolution by the Knights Hospitaller, a monastic brotherhood that started off in the eleventh century as an organisation providing medical care to pilgrims in Jerusalem. With the start of the Crusades they began to get involved in the fighting alongside their great rivals, the Knights Templar. Like the Templars they became one of the great commercial enterprises of the Middle Ages but unlike the Templars they seem to have stuck, at least partly, to their roots in providing medical care, even to their enemies.

With the collapse of the Crusades they moved first to Cyprus and Rhodes and then to Malta, where they stayed until after the French Revolution, the "Last Crusaders" surviving anachronistically into the start of the era of the Nation State.

The order finally disintegrated as a united organisation but its distant descendants are still around today. One of these is the Sovereign Order of the Knights of Malta which claims to be about 10,500 strong worldwide. This is recognised under international law as a "sovereign entity" – a landless mini-state in fact – with diplomatic representatives in 90 countries. Its status as a sovereign entity was underlined in 1994 when it was granted "Permanent Observer" to the United Nations. It is a lay organisation within the Catholic Church and has been associated in some quarters with the conservative right.

Many members of the order of the Knights Hospitaller came to Britain and it lives on in the guise of the Most Venerable Order of Saint John, an order of the British Crown, with the Queen as Sovereign Head. The emblem common to all these descendents of the Hospitallers is the parent order's own symbol, the Maltese Cross. This will be familiar to all as the emblem of another offshoot of the Hospitallers, the St John's Ambulance, a voluntary medical organisation echoing the origins of its distant ancestor.

Wyke

The path descends into a dip in the cliffs. This is Hayburn Wyke, now a nature reserve and owned by the National Trust. A wyke is a generic name for an inlet usually carrying a stream which forms a break in the cliffs in this part of the world.

Part of the citation by English Nature for Hayburn Wyke reads..

"The Middle Jurassic cliffs at Hayburn Wyke are overlain by a thick deposit of boulder clay. The Hayburn Beck, which falls onto the beach in a waterfall, has carved a channel through the rocks to expose the Hayburn Wyke plant bed. The plant bed forms part of the Cloughton Formation of the Middle Jurassic and contains a rich fossil fauna, comprising sixty species, dominated by cycads. Of particular interest is Hepaticites haiburnensis, a marchantiaceous liverwort, known only from this locality. The geological interest of this site has not yet been fully evaluated, but it is without question an outstanding fossil plant locality."

Hayburn Wyke used to have a railway station and nearby there is a small stone circle. A report in the early 20th century says that there were *"about fifteen monoliths making up the circle, all lying flat on the ground, so that in the summer they are very much overgrown with rank grass and low bushes. This was probably the burial-place of some prehistoric chief, but no mound remains."*

The Cleveland Way doesn't actually hit the beach but turns right just off the bridge, back up through the undergrowth and up again to the cliffs. But the short detour of a few yards is worth a look because just to the left of this picture the beck splits into two and cascades over a drop of about 20 feet making a rather pretty double waterfall.

During World War II Hayburn Wyke was "home", for the months of February to May 1941, to 'D' Company of the 7th Battalion of The Loyal Regiment (North Lancashire) which had been allocated coastal defence duties. These resourceful men were, by and large, left to their own devices with whatever weapons could be had and, with no accommodation supplied, had to make their homes by digging holes in the cliffs. It was a winter with many hard frosts and there were casualties from exposure.

Algae

Algal taxonomy is built on shifting sands, but here are the four colours....

Most chlorophyta (green algae, pictured) are aquatic, but some types can live on the surface of snow, on tree trunks or in soil. They are typically coloured green to yellow-green.

Phaeophyta (brown algae) are almost entirely marine, and some are so dominating they can form small-scale forests. Their colour ranges from pale beige to almost black, and in size from microscopic to several metres long.

Most Rhodophyta (red algae) are found in the sea although a few are found in freshwater. They are usually multi-cellular and grow attached to rocks or other algae.

Cyanobacteria (blue-green algae) are primitive organisms lacking a true nucleus. Although they are bacteria, they are photosynthetic and are classed with algae. They played a vital role in raising the free oxygen levels in the atmosphere of early Earth. They have been found in both freezing Antarctic lakes and hot springs.

Most of the seaweeds we see are green algae and the kelps are from the brown group. They have many economic uses, mainly in the foodstuffs industries and some of them are eaten in their own right, particularly in Japan, China and Hawaii but also as dulse in Ireland and Scotland.

Alginates derived from the brown algae are used in ice cream manufacture, shaving cream, latex rubbers, material for dental impressions, and paints. They are also, echoes of the old alum trade, used in textiles to help conserve dyes.

Agar, derived from red algae, is used in a wide variety of industries. Pharmaceutically it is used as a base for slow release drugs, a growth medium for bacteria, in cosmetics and photographic film, shoe polish, shaving soaps and hand creams. In the food industry it's used as a gelatin substitute, an anti-drying agent in breads and pastries, the manufacture of processed cheeses mayonnaise, puddings, creams and jellies. There's more to seaweed than meets the eye.

Seaweed clad boulders at Hayburn Wyke

Path

The path back to the clifftop from Hayburn Wyke passes through a small wood where for once you might actually have to look for the waymarks and you may even manage a wrong turning. I did.

It is an old trail of some sort or other, bounded by a dry stone wall. An account written in 1890 reports that Hayburn Wyke was *"much resorted to by pleasure seekers. There is a station, and a hotel and farm, where excellent accommodation can be had. The grounds are extensive, and in the woods we find such forest trees as the oak, ash, birch, pine, &c. The beck, falling over the rock, forms beautiful cascades. The guide says 'Hayburn Wyke, with its rugged sea beach, picturesque waterfalls, sheltered glens, and lovely woodlands, affords most romantic and charmingly secluded walks.'"* The obvious effort at engineering the pathway points to a use more substantial than pleasure seekers' woodland walks, but no pointers are given as to its former use.

Again, extracted from the words of the English Nature SSSI citation...

"Deciduous woodland covers the slopes above the cliff shelf and extends some way up Hayburn Wyke Beck, merging into a mixed broad leaved and conifer woodland. The canopy is dominated by oak (both Quercus petraea and Q. robur) with ash, sycamore, birch and elm. There are several standards of large-leaved lime. The understorey of shrubs includes hazel, holly and goat willow, and there is a rich ground flora with sanicle, opposite-leaved golden saxifrage, wood millet, male fern, lady fern Athyrium and hart's tongue fern. The damp conditions favour mosses and liverworts." There are also many species of fungi including the appetisingly named Stinkhorn.

Near where the Cleveland Way emerges from the woodland and takes a sharp left you can follow the footpath on for not much more than 50 yards, take a right turn before you get to the old railway line and about two hundred yards along the path you'll find the Hayburn Wyke Hotel. Nicely situated about half way between Ravenscar and Scalby Mills it's the only watering hole within easy striking distance of the clifftops on this stretch of the walk.

The overgrown path with moss covered stone walls out of Hayburn Wyke

Cloughton

Back on the clifftops again we enter the parish of Cloughton. Cloughton, once known as Clotune, is more or less attached to the neighbouring village of Burniston and is separated from the urban development of Scarborough by about a mile of countryside. Cloughton village itself is situated about half a mile inland from the Cleveland Way where the path reaches Cloughton Wyke.

Cloughton was, unsurprisingly, rumoured once to have been a centre for smuggling. Contraband was landed at Cloughton Wyke with the obligatory secret tunnel, in this case supposedly ending in the Manor House.

Above the village lies an abandoned sandstone quarry which supplied the stone for Scarborough Castle.

The 15th century cruciform church of St. Mary the Virgin at Cloughton was built in the early Decorated style and was once a chapel-of-ease. Substantial restoration was carried out in the late 19th century but there was quite a lot of the original stonework preserved. The only monument in the church, fixed to the south wall near the chancel is a marble tablet with arms on a gilt background which tells us that "William Brown, and Priscilla, his wife, lived long and comfortably in wedlock for 70 and 3 years. Hee dyed 1698, aged 96; shee dyed 1698, aged 91 years". Probably the only incidence of a recorded platinum wedding couple in the villages alongside the Cleveland Way. It requires some thought to imagine the life of a man born an Elizabethan when Shakespeare was writing his plays and who died nine years after the bloodless revolution in the reign of William III.

The vicarage was built in 1876 at a cost of £1,500, defrayed by the Ecclesiastical Commissioners. Little did they know that a hundred and twenty five years later its incumbent would be an ex-policeman and a world famous author.

In an interesting example of co-operative venture, the villagers researched and published a book about the 2000 year history of their village. The moving force behind the project, Harold Whitfield, died in 1999 but the Cloughton Millennium Committee finished the work as part of their celebrations.

The Cleveland Way looking back over Hayburn Wyke

Shadowmancer

The Cleveland Way continues its route hugging the cliff tops above the rocky shoreline.

Cloughton's main claim to international fame is that it was the home of the Rev G.P. Taylor, unlikely best selling author of Shadowmancer.

I say unlikely because after being a bit of a rebel in his youth he left it all behind to take up ministry in the Church of England. He has some harsh words both for the old time traditionalists and the evangelicals, commenting that "The ministry in the eighteenth century was too often peopled by third sons of the gentry who had nothing better to do. They weren't particularly spiritual, let alone pleasant. Many were local tyrants who exploited their congregation via the tithing system. I am making a point about the abuse of religious power."

He lectures in the paranormal and the occult and has attracted some criticism: "I have had the odd letter threatening me with the fires of hell for promoting witchcraft. This is nonsense of course. The book is about good winning over evil. Most evangelicals would not know a witch if one sat next to them on the subway."

Graham had been a policeman but had to resign from the police force after he was a victim of an assault that left him deaf in one ear.

The international success of Shadowmancer came as a bit of a surprise, not least to the author, who had sold his motorbike to pay to get it published. These early copies are now worth money. He asked the church treasurer to shift some of the last copies of the first edition to generate some church funds. Twelve were sold at the parish bring-and-buy sale at the original price of £5.99. "I had assumed he knew that they are now worth £1,000 each", said the author.

Now plain Mr. G.P. Taylor, having resigned his church position because of ill health, he was himself the author of a second literary mishap when moving out of his church accommodation. To dispose of some old rubbish he decided to build a bonfire. Unfortunately some of the rubbish turned out to be the early drafts of his first three novels, including the only extant draft of Shadowmancer. He was pictured in newspapers clutching the charred remains of his masterpieces looking not a little crestfallen.

The cliffs at Cloughton Wyke

North Bay

Hugging the clifftops closely the Cleveland Way passes Cloughton Wyke, out to Long Nab, down a dip into Crook Ness then gradually downhill to Scalby Ness and the pub at Scalby Mills. At low tide the rock patterns swirl and crack with the geometric patterns testimony to the geological forces that formed them over 150 million years ago.

Scalby Mills marks the start of the Tabular Hills Walk which meanders its way back to Helmsley by way of forestry commission land, the southern edge of the moors near Fylingdales and the Hole of Horcum, through Levisham, Newton-on-Rawncliffe, Cropton, Hutton-le-Hole, Appleton-le-Moors, Gillamoor, Fadmoor and Carlton, villages which skirt the southern boundary of the North York Moors National Park, before dropping back into Helmsley by way of a forestry plantation to the north.

On reaching Scalby there is a welcoming pub and a beck where you can have a splodge around in the sea with the North Bay sweeping round to the headland, itself surmounted by the ruined castle. The white pyramids here post date the Giza variants by some four thousand years and instead of kingly tombs or repositories of secrets from an alien civilisation (you choose) ours here are home to the aquatic creatures of the Scarborough Sea Life Centre.

The North Bay is Scarborough's quieter side, a beach with donkey rides, an open air pool and Peasholm Park, a venue for regular scale model sea battles.

The Cleveland Way takes a break when it meets Scarborough and if you want you can get the open topped bus to the Spa at the end of South Bay where the trail picks up again for the final stretch along the cliffs to Filey. If you have a mind and the inclination for a bit of steam then there's a miniature railway which will take you a bit further down along the bay from Scalby to the little railway station by the swimming pool opposite Peasholm.

The headland is now protected by the same gneiss rock from Norway that has already been installed at Staithes, Runswick Bay and Whitby to act as a first line in the sea defences. The traffic along here is usually quite heavy and my own preference is for the gentle uphill walk to the castle and down again into South Bay. There are at least three advantages I can think of to taking this route – less traffic, a visit to the castle and the view from the headland, particularly from the castle battlements, back to Ravenscar and right along south eastwards to the Cleveland Way's clifftop path to Filey.

270

Gaveston

Home to an Iron Age settlement and a Roman signal station, now believed to be situated on the edge of the cliff under the castle ruins, and raided in 1066 by Harald Haardrade, it was not until the reign of King Stephen that this site hosted a stone fortification.

In 1140 during King Stephen's reign William de Gros, Count of Albermarle and Holderness, who was on the winning side at the battle of the Standards near Northallerton, started to build a castle here on this promontory. In 1154 it was taken over by Henry II who built the great tower and probably the curtain walls. His son King John visited the castle on four occasions and the fortifications were strengthened during John's reign. It remained a royal possession until Stuart times.

In 1312 Edward II's "favourite" Piers Gaveston was besieged here by the sensitive barons he had offended by his outrageous behaviour. Near to starvation he surrendered, only to be taken away and executed, much to the King's consternation. In 1557 Thomas Stafford was so maddened by the marriage of Queen Mary to Philip of Spain that he and a group cunningly disguised as peasants attacked the castle. After only a week Stafford was captured and sent to the Tower of London.

Sir Hugh Cholmley held Scarborough castle for the Royalists in 1645 but he switched sides to the Parliamentarians. They then put colonel Boynton in charge but he did the opposite and switched to the Royalists, so the Parliamentarians had to do it all again in 1648. The castle was wrecked by Cromwell after the Civil War and its position on the very edge of the cliff has meant a great deal more has been lost to erosion. Most of the ruins that have survived, including the keep, date from the twelfth century, from Henry II's time.

George Fox, the founder of the Quakers and one time frequenter of this section of the Yorkshire coast, was imprisoned here during Oliver Cromwell's Commonwealth in 1665.

In 1914 the castle was bombarded by two German cruisers and the barracks, built in 1756 after the Jacobite uprising, were destroyed.

Approaching Scarborough Castle from North Bay

Spa

Passing down from the castle to the South Bay you will see the church of St Mary. This was once owned by the Cistercians and dates from the twelfth century. Much altered in its time and damaged by the Civil War and erosion, it is the last resting place of Anne Brontë, who died in Scarborough on 28 May 1849 aged 28.

Passing along the front with its garish amusements, rides and fish and chip parlours on one side and the beach lovers on the other, we arrive back to the Cleveland Way proper near the Spa.

The Spa itself can trace its origins back to 1626 when a Mrs Tomyzin Farrer claimed that the local spring water had health giving properties. Dr Robert Wittie published "Scarborough Spaw" in 1660 advocating the waters as a cure for all ills. He recommended that the waters were best drunk mid-May to mid-September and before long the spa circuit added Scarborough to Bath, Buxton and Tunbridge Wells. The first cisterns were built in 1698 by the Corporation and "Spaw House" was built in 1700 by one Dickie Dickinson.

Subsidence and storms took their toll over the following 125 years and in 1825 it was very nearly washed away altogether. In 1826 the Spaw was taken over by the Cliff Bridge company, founded specifically to build the bridge which you will have passed on the way. 1826 was the year when the "Spaw" became the "Spa".

There have been many alterations and additions since then but it remains with its regular concerts (seating being laid out in the morning here) and conference facilities. The biggest investment of £3m transformed the sagging Grand Hall into a regenerated version of the venue as it was in its heyday in Victorian times. A further £2m was spent in a project that was completed in 1984 to build a new east facade, Promenade lounge and mezzanine bar. Two years later saw a further £600,000 for the ballroom, catering facilities and passenger lift. Let's hope the sea can be persuaded to give the £5.6m investment a bit of a chance before the whole lot collapses into it, when it will join the missing bits of the castle and the Holbeck Hall Hotel.

The Spa on the end of Scarborough South Bay

275

Scarborough Fair

Scarborough Fair originated from a charter granted by King Henry III on 22 January 1253. The charter, which gave Scarborough many privileges, stated "*The Burgesses and their heirs forever may have a yearly fayre in the Borough, to continue from the Feast of the Assumption of the Blessed Virgin Mary until the Feast of St Michael next following*". Traditionally the fair proclamation began 'Lord, Gentlemen and Loons. You're welcome to our toons until St Michael's Day, but tolls and customs pay from Latter Lammas Day.'

The 45-day Fayre was held annually and became internationally famous. Merchants came from Norway, Denmark, the Baltic and as far away as the Ottoman Empire. Each stallholder had to pay 2d to the Burgesses.

However, it caused problems with the neighbours. In 1256 Scarborough quarrelled with Filey, Sherburn and Brompton, who each had their own fairs. The Burgesses pleaded to the King's Court to get them abolished, claiming they were taking trade away from Scarborough. Scarborough won and the competition ceased.

A similar long running battle with Seamer ended up with a short lived Scarborough win in 1602, but after much closing and re-opening Seamer's market eventually prevailed and Scarborough Fair ended in 1788.

The song was made internationally famous in 1968 with Simon and Garfunkel's "The Graduate" soundtrack. Performers of English folk songs use a version very similar to this one which was collected by Frank Kitson in the late 19th Century and sung by Martin Carthy and Ewan MacColl and Peggy Seeger. The song is certainly much older than that and presumably predates 1788 when the last fair was held. It chimes strongly with the old riddle songs and the second line of each verse – Parsley, Sage, Rosemary and Thyme very possibly holds references to the magical properties attributed to herbs by the old sorcerers who used them in their potions and spells. These particular ones are associated with death and potions for people wanting to ward off the evil eye. The song then becomes a challenge from an evil entity to a young girl, setting impossible tasks, with the girl's fate dependent on her replies.

Collapse

Once again the path takes the high ground on the last stretch to Filey Brigg. Just south of Scarborough there is a large area which looks like it has been scooped out of the cliffside. In fact, that is more or less what happened on a dramatic morning in June 1993.

Holbeck Hall Hotel was a four-star establishment standing about 210ft above sea level on South Cliff built in 1880 by Charles Alderson Smith who at that time owned about 9 acres of land extending to the sea. On the morning of June 3rd 1993 it looked out over an expanse of lawn to panoramic views of the North Sea. Three days later the lawn had disappeared and the ground had collapsed under the entire seaward wing of the hotel as a result of a massive land-slip which took place in four stages. The rest of the hotel was unsafe and had to be demolished. The good news was that as it had been a gradual process everybody had been evacuated and there were no casualties. The whole spectacle was filmed and broadcast worldwide on television.

The live broadcast of the spectacular collapse was a dramatic indication of what will happen to much of the clifftop section of the Cleveland Way. Parts of the original path have gone for ever and other bits are dropping off at regular intervals. However, such inconveniences are at worst temporary as the Way will continue to exist, albeit in a landward progression as time and tide take their relentless toll on the Yorkshire coast. The natural erosion of the cliffs does have one up side, though. As bits drop off the cliffs we sometimes get a new crop of fossils exposed.

By this time you can see the end of the path at Filey Brigg stretching out ahead of you along the coast. The path is fairly level and easy walking but here, as before, care is a requirement on much of the walk especially when it's slippery underfoot and the winds are blowing from the west.

The path passes above Johnny Flinton's Harbour, on occasion a favoured spot for naturists. Just so you know.

We descend a little but not all the way to the beach then up again to the clifftop above the sweeping Cayton Bay. Cayton village, a mile or so inland, has a very rare, and very fortunate, distinction.

Twice Thankful

IN FLANDERS FIELDS the poppies blow
Between the crosses, row on row,
That mark our place, and in the sky
The larks, still bravely singing, fly
Scarce heard amid the guns below.

We are the Dead. Short days ago
We lived, felt dawn, saw sunset glow,
Loved and were loved, and now we lie
In Flanders fields.

Take up our quarrel with the foe:
To you from failing hands we throw
The torch; be yours to hold it high.
If ye break faith with us who die
We shall not sleep, though poppies grow
In Flanders fields.

This poem was written by Major John McCrae, a Canadian army doctor, in the Ypres salient in 1915, after a young friend of his, Lieut. Alexis Helmer of Ottawa, was killed by a shell on 2 May, 1915. In the absence of the chaplain McCrae had conducted the burial and he wrote the poem in five minutes the following day, sitting on the back of an ambulance.

The author didn't like it and so he threw it away, but it was retrieved by another officer who sent it to newspapers in England. It was rejected by the Spectator but published by Punch.

In 1921, someone who knew McCrae's poem wore a poppy to commemorate the war dead and sold them to friends to raise funds for ex-servicemen. Poppies then came to represent the war dead and of course are now the ubiquitous emblem of Remembrance in Britain.

The number of "Thankful Villages" is usually given as 32 but there are some differences of opinion as both to the definition and the number, which is sometimes given as high as 54. There is also a suggestion that there may be more but that the 32 are the ones who have actually commemorated the fact in stone.

Cayton has double cause for thanks because not only did they get all their young men back after the first World War, they repeated the trick the next time around in World War II. This is one of the very few places in Britain with such luck.

ΘΑΛΑΣΣΑ

This is the view awaiting you as you round Lebberston Cliff.

The sea is the next door neighbour for about half the journey. Some interesting ocean facts:

The sea constitutes nearly 71% of the earth's surface, holds more than 97% of all the water and the average temperature is just over 2°C. The top ten feet holds as much heat as the whole atmosphere and the average depth is more than 2.5 miles. It provides 99 percent of the Earth's living space and more than 90% of this habitat exists in the deep sea known as the abyss. Less than 10% of this living space has been explored. The deepest point in the sea is more than a mile deeper than Everest is high. The water pressure at this point (the Mariana Trench near the Philippines) is more than 8 tons per square inch – the equivalent of one person trying to hold 50 jumbo jets. The Antarctic ice sheet that forms and melts over the ocean every year is almost twice the area of the United States. The cold, saline water that forms off the coast of Iceland can be found in the North Pacific about 1000 years later. One cubic mile of sea water contains about 30,000,000 tons of salt.

The Gulf Stream which is responsible for the UK's mild climate flows from the Gulf of Mexico at a rate nearly 300 times faster than the typical flow of the Amazon, the world's largest river. The world's seas contain nearly 20 million tons of gold. A single mouthful of seawater may contain millions of bacterial cells, hundreds of thousands of phytoplankton and tens of thousands of zooplankton. Tasty, eh? Yum yum.

The Athenians were a seafaring city state in the fourth century BC but after the Peloponnesian War with Sparta, the Greeks found themselves with nobody to fight. So 10,000 of them joined up as mercenaries in the service of Cyrus the Younger, who intended to seize the throne of Persia from his brother, Artaxerxes II. Though Cyrus' army won its battle in Babylon, Cyrus was killed in the battle and with the expedition over the Greeks' thoughts turned to home. After a long march they finally arrived at the Black Sea. After so many hardships in foreign landlocked battles the cry went up from the sea-loving soldiers – one word. "ΘΑΛΑΣΣΑ!" (pronounced thalassa) – THE SEA!.

Skardi

Scarborough is still clearly visible behind us. According to a medieval Icelandic saga – the Kormakssaga – two Icelandic Viking brothers by the name of Kormak and Thorgils were the first men to "establish the fort called Skardaborg". It was named after the nickname of one of its founders – Thorgils was called Skardi, meaning hare-lipped and pronounced "Scarthi", by his brother, who may or may not have been nicknamed split lipped when presumably Thorgils took exception to Kormak's sense of humour. It is now generally accepted that the name Skardaborg, which has come down to us as Scarborough, means "the fort belonging to Skardi". The Borough part is a derivative of the Scandinavian "Borg" or fortification. Scarborough is possibly the only town in Britain named after a human physical abnormality.

Kormakssaga has more to say about these brothers. Kormak was a talented poet, as we can infer from his naming witticisms, and was described as a wild man with black curly hair. Thorgils on the other hand was taciturn and easygoing. Both men apparently shared a taste for adventure and plundering around the coasts of Britain and Ireland. They were in the service of King Harald Grafeld, King of Norway between the years 960-965AD. They accompanied the king's expedition to Bjarmaland or Permia in northern Russia in 966AD and the expedition to England followed almost immediately. In 966 they decided to make the sheltered waters of the south bay their base and built the fort. This dates the foundation of the continuous inhabitation of Scarborough to the middle of the tenth century and in all probability to 966 or 967. Kormak was killed in 967 while raiding in Scotland. It is interesting to speculate whether the Scots found his talent for nicknames amusing.

The parts of the walk where it passes away from the clifftops into meadowland are home to a wide variety of plant and insect life. Butterflies abound and there are many species of wild flowers including several types of orchid. The many sections which haven't been manicured by the landowners make slightly more difficult walking but the difference in the insect and plant wildlife is striking.

Plant aficionados wishing to extend their knowledge beyond the mere dusting possible in this book would be well advised to seek out 'Wildflowers of the North Yorkshire Coast' by Nan Sykes (ISBN 1 904622 02 X). Lots of information about the subject with plenty of colour photographs.

Sheer Cliffs

The warning sign only says half of it. The cliffs are only dangerous if you are silly and wander off the track. Don't stray out to the edge – keep to the path and you'll be fine. It has been said by wiser men than me that the length of the drop doesn't matter just so long as you don't fall off. And you won't if you stay on the path. Not rocket science, as the saying goes.

Inland we pass caravanning and campsite country with – to name but three – the Lebberston Touring Park, the Flower of May (also at Lebberston) and the extensive Blue Dolphin Caravan Park, bordering the Cleveland Way are along this stretch. Some of the sites are quiet and others go to great lengths to inform their potential customers that they aren't.

Lebberston and Gristhorpe villages lie to the west of the path. The Gristhorpe fossil beds are especially noted for their plant fossils as well as the ammonites and shells found in abundance elsewhere along this stretch of the Way. "Gristhorpe Man", a Bronze Age tree trunk burial, is an exhibit in the Rotunda Museum in Scarborough.

We're now on the finishing stretch of the Cleveland Way and the route eventually moves inland from the cliff edge and the views are to the west.

The Way now passes atop the end of the sandstone cliffs which stretch back to Saltburn, broken by Wykes and picturesque villages . To the south past Filey the sheer cliffs are chalk. The difference is obvious – the oranges and reds of the Cleveland Way give way to the off-white sheer coast which ends around the Flamborough headland at Bridlington.

The coastline begins to soften from the vertical cliffs and takes on a gentler aspect where erosion has resulted in steep slopes rather than sheer drops. The character of the Way becomes more gentle and less grand, more gentle country stroll than wild clifftop vistas.

We're nearly at the end and it's been a delight. The variations we've seen, the history, the geology, the flora, the fauna and above all the huge variations in territory and scenery all go to make the Cleveland Way a uniquely varied trail.

Descent

The final stretch is a leisurely stroll and as easy a section of the walk as has been. Nearing the end it's maybe the place for a little idle speculation on a couple of things passed on the trip.

We have quite a detailed understanding of why the Cleveland Way looks like it does. The geological forces that formed the underlying structure are well understood and we know a great deal about the way man's activities, particularly in the extractive industries, have altered its appearance from the jet mine spoils to the iron-contaminated streams to the alum shale remnants. We've seen how Henry VIII left ruins in the place of large monasteries and how fishermen and smugglers built the villages on the coast and which are now to no small extent in the hands of second homers and holiday letters.

What would have happened to the monastic buildings if Henry hadn't quarrelled with Rome? Possibly the best thing that could have been wished for is that they turned into what the Spaniards have done with several of their own unused monastic buildings and made them into the English version of the Parador hotels. Maybe they would be retreats and health farms for the wealthy. I somehow doubt that many, if any at all, would have survived into the 21st century as religious institutions.

And what of the 96% of the universe that they're looking for under Boulby? Who knows what the implications of that are. Our minds struggle to grasp the scale of the observable universe and then we go and find out that everything we know so far is less than one twentieth of what our calculations tell us must actually be there.

And who was it that found out, hundreds of years before Dalton's atomic theory and the transformation from alchemy to chemistry, that by taking the shales from the same beds as certain fossils, building a fire under them, letting it burn for a year, treating the residue with barrels of urine, settling the mixture out, deciding the optimum moment for crystallisation by floating an egg, collecting the white crystals that ensue and boiling them up with wool or silk it would enable the treated fabrics to hold on to their vegetable dyestuffs after washing?

The path along the cliff edge approaching Filey

The End

The end of the Cleveland Way is marked, as is the beginning, by a stone carved with the National Trail symbol (the acorn) and some of the names of the places passed on the path. Filey Brigg, a rocky outcrop jutting into the North Sea, is below and Filey itself is about half a mile to the west. You don't get any points for walking it but there isn't much of an option.

The view over Filey Bay to Flamborough is tempting, but the Cleveland Way is sensible to stop where it does.

The end of the Cleveland Way also marks the beginning (or end) of the Yorkshire Wolds Way, so if you haven't had enough then maybe this is worth a look. At 79 miles it is shorter than the Cleveland Way and less dramatic in its extremes. It passes through some of the best preserved ancient villages in the country, including the remarkable preserved and deserted mediaeval village of Wharram Percy. Starting at Filey you end up on the Humber at Hessle, more or less underneath the Humber Bridge. Usually the guides to this route start at Hessle and finish at Filey Brigg but no doubt the conquerors of the Cleveland Way will be able to cope with a bit of reverse engineering.

The distance travelled on the Cleveland Way is, officially, 110 miles, but if you've detoured and broken the journey (not many people do it without stopping) you will have walked a few miles more than that.

The Cleveland Way doesn't take in Filey, nor does it include Filey Brigg, but I'd be willing to bet that many people finishing the National Trail will take the detour to investigate this striking promontory with the expansive views over the chalk Bempton Cliffs, home to huge populations of sea birds in the breeding season. There is a coastal path along Bempton Cliffs but it isn't connected to the Cleveland Way – it starts at Speeton and ends the other side of Flamborough Head.

When we finished the Cleveland Way my wife and I found our way to Filey bus station to get back to Scarborough. The bus had "Scarborough via Hessle" on the destination board and we thought this unlikely from Filey as a trip through Hessle would entail something of a detour in completely the wrong direction. So we decided to ask the driver if he was going to Scarborough. He took a look outside, glanced at the sky and said "It looks like a nice day. Why not?"

The end of the Way and the cliffs down to Flamborough